THE
BLACK
MZUNGU

A MEMOIR & TRAVELOGUE

THE
BLACK
MZUNGU

A MEMOIR & TRAVELOGUE

A SAGA OF SELF-DISCOVERY, LOVE, IDENTITY, AND
TRIUMPH IN TANZANIA, EAST AFRICA

ALEXANDRIA K. OSBORNE, PH.D

Niyah Publishing

Detroit, MI

NIYAH PUBLISHING
WWW.ENLIVENYOURSOUL.COM

Niyah Publishing

Publisher's Note: This is a memoir. Some names have been changed to protect the identity of the individual.

Editor: Nadirah Angail
Cover Design: Focsi

Managing Editor: Zarinah El-Amin Naeem

The Black Mzungu/ Alexandria K. Osborne. -- 1st ed.

ISBN 978-0-9822215-7-0

Library of Congress Control Number: 2014921651

Printed in the United States

To the loved ones I left behind:

Zubayda, Nuri, and Camila

PREFACE

I never thought of myself as a writer. Growing up, I was a student of the sciences and struggled in required English and writing classes. Supervisors, who had nothing else to criticize during performance reviews, always mentioned developing my writing skills.

Later, propelled by all of the writing required in my doctoral program, and mandatory journals for my fellowship in Tanzania, I finally gained the courage to write and share with a wider audience.

After arriving in Tanzania, I began sharing personal updates via email. People actually seemed interested in reading about my experiences; after all, it was cheaper than a plane ticket to East Africa. After a while, trying to be less invasive of people's inboxes, like billions, I turned to social media. With a $100 camera and time, my journaling became lengthy Facebook posts. I was encouraged by so many from my past: an elementary school teacher, old classmates, ex-colleagues, friends, brothers and sisters in faith, friends I had only met in Facebook, and family.

Social media has its purpose. It is a place to galvanize people for common causes and to share and discuss the topics of the day. However, it has its limitations; and, through it, I could not concisely explain to my loved ones the history of where I came from and how I arrived in this place. Hence, this book was written with the desire to leave a legacy for my daughter and grandchildren. It is my story of adaptation to the people, land and country I learned to call home.

While it seemed as if I had been going to school all my life, college and grad school were nothing like what I was beginning to embark upon. Little did I know that for the second half-century of my life, my education would come in a much more organic fashion. During this journey, I began to really understand what Abraham Maslow meant when he said, "All of life is education and everybody is a teacher and everybody is forever a pupil." In Tanzania, I am a student every day and a teacher every day.

The following is my account of the things I've experienced. There are good times and bad times, rewarding times and trying times, funny times and mundane times, but it is all my truth as a mzungu in Tanzania.

Note: Mzungu is the Swahili word for wanderer, but it is most often used to denote a person of European descent or a foreigner.

*Chapters are organized around a series of non-chronological events that are sometimes connected and sometimes not. Some names have been changed to protect the identity of the individual. The glossary at the end can assist readers with abbreviations and non-English terms which are italicized in the text.

Visit www.theblackmzungu.com for a full list of group discussion questions and to view the picture gallery.

CONTENTS

MAP OF TANZANIA[1]

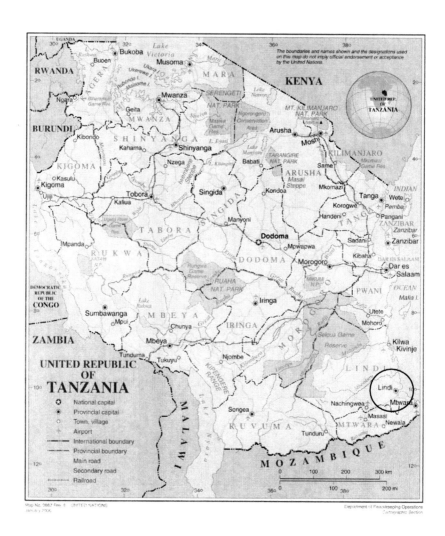

[1] Courtesy of Sameer Kermalli. Adapted from United Nations Cartographic Section, Department of Field Support. Map of the United Republic of Tanzania. (2006). Retrieved from http://www.un.org/Depts/Cartographic/map/profile/tanzania.pdf

CHAPTER 1

MOVING TO THE MOTHERLAND

Have you ever found yourself thinking, "There has to be more to life?" In 2009, my daughter was grown and on her own; I had a great job and was finishing up my doctoral studies in Management. Still, I felt an anxiousness about my future. I wanted more, and this time I wanted to define it on my own terms.

I had a blessed life by all means, yet professionally, I felt I had peaked. I remember saying to myself, "2010 will be a year of change." I felt it and was prepared for it. Seeking something new, I discovered that my employer organized international fellowships for employees. As a part of their social responsibility initiative, international non-governmental organizations (NGOs)—at no cost to them—were able to select from a pool of well-trained company staff to come and work with them for a 6-month period. Our company reimbursed the NGO and employee for all expenses incurred except food. The idea was that employees would receive a rich experience that, ideally, would make them better employees upon their return; and the NGOs would have access to top-level trained staff. The program sounded and felt right, so I applied.

As part of the fellowship selection process, I had interviews with several NGOs, including offices located in Rwanda and Ghana, but Tanzania felt right. I do not know why. When I got word I was selected, I gave credit to all of my North African experience. I believe I would not have had a chance to be selected without it. My ex-husband is a Libyan American. As a result, and despite the sanctions against what the George W. Bush administration labeled as "beyond the axis of evil," I had visited my Libyan in-laws nine times over an 18-year time period. Escorting my daughter on her summer vacation, most times without my ex-husband, these journeys to North Africa were quite adventurous at times and often required creativity to reach my final destination.

I have taken the ferry from Malta, traveled by land and air from Tunisia, and rendezvoused with in-laws in Egypt. My American passport has been confiscated in Libya on at least one occasion. Another time, I was told I could not leave with my daughter until she had a Libyan passport. Traveling by land from Tunisia, I was even mistakenly waved through a Libyan checkpoint by Gaddafi's young security forces who assumed I was a Libyan woman, only to find out upon my departure that I did not have the required entry stamp. During those 18 years, I was searched and interrogated multiple times by various security forces, both friends and foes of my native country.

Nevertheless, I became very comfortable with the people of North Africa, and despite a deteriorating marriage, I decided to take advantage of my unique access to the country of Libya by choosing it as the location to undertake my PhD dissertation research. In retrospect, it helped me understand what laid ahead in Tanzania.

Being a fair-complexioned African-American Muslim, I fit into the North African landscape well. But emotionally, I was spent. Despite my warm relationship with my ex-in-laws and acceptance because of our common faith, there were still language and cultural challenges. And although this was before the Arab Spring, the political volatility of Libya and its relationship with the West made for a precarious travel environment. Like many, I had experienced betrayal and disappointment in my personal life. So once my ex-husband and I ended our 24-year marriage, I was more than ready to write a new chapter on the next phase of my life.

Like many African Americans, I fantasized about setting foot on the land my ancestors were removed from during the biggest forced migration of a people from their homeland. Thanks to Alex Haley, some of us imagine being greeted by our distant cousins as Mr. Haley was greeted by his relatives in the village Kunta Kinte, his forebear, was captured from centuries earlier. However, few of us have the resources, skills or will to take on such a massive research project. It was enough for me just to set foot in sub-Saharan Africa. It did not matter that most recorded history of the slave trade to the Americas occurred in West Africa. East Africa would do. It was with much anticipation that I looked forward to visiting sub-Saharan Africa, the Motherland, for the first time.

While preparing for my trip to Tanzania, I exchanged many emails with the NGO officers. I noticed that with each subsequent email, more and more names were added to the recipient list: first the American country director, then the assistant country director, then the program manager I would be reporting to, then the manager of administration, and finally the logistic and transport officer. The latter would be responsible for obtaining my Tanzanian work permit from immigration, finding my housing and picking me up from the airport. The logistics officer was the first Muslim name I saw in the correspondence. For some strange reason, I had a weird feeling when I noticed that name.

I landed in Tanzania's largest city, Dar es Salaam (we call it Dar for short), in August 2009 to begin my six-month fellowship. I was ready to begin defining the next few years of my life. Tanzania is located on the eastern coast of Africa. It shares borders with Mozambique, Malawi, the Democratic Republic of Congo, Zambia, Uganda, Rwanda and Kenya. Tanzania is home to the Serengeti and

Selous Reserves. Lake Victoria, which feeds East Africa's lifeline, the Nile River, supplies a livelihood for many fishermen in the north. Professional climbers and tourists alike flock to Tanzania to climb Africa's tallest peak, Kilimanjaro. The semi-precious stone tanzanite can only be found at the foot of Kilimanjaro.

Most visitors come to Tanzania and its northern neighbor Kenya to experience its game parks and see God's wildlife in its natural habitat. Being a large coastal country, it has cool mountains, grasslands, dense forests and a humid southern coast. I did not know at the time that the latter would become my new home and maybe last home.

Tanzania has hosted refugees from its less-stable neighbors for decades. The influx of refugees led to the arrival of well-meaning international aid agencies. However, even without the occasional refugee crisis, most of Tanzania's 40 million people, 75% of which live in rural villages, survive on less than $2 per day. Like most Africans, partly due to mismanagement, corruption, and a failure of trickledown economics, they have not benefited from its country's rich natural resources. The Tanzanian people were colonized by Germans, the Arab Sultans and the British. Its history has led to a mixture of faiths that, for most part, live peacefully among each other. Today it is a democracy with an elected president and parliament.

I had scheduled my flight to arrive one week before the start of the Muslim fasting month of Ramadan. My thinking was that one week would be enough time to adapt to the time change, establish the routine of fasting from dawn to sunset and find a mosque for *tarawee*, the late night prayers that occur only during Ramadan. I assumed finding places to pray and practice Islam would be easy. With Ramadan so close, my immediate thoughts focused on establishing a routine for the month. Yet, there were still so many new things to absorb.

Maybe it was a combination of the mental preparation, emotional readiness and physical maturity, but the culture shock and move to Tanzania was much less dramatic than my move from New York City to Kalamazoo, Michigan in 1980 at the age of 23. This is not to say that I was not surprised to see how so many in the world live, but my cultural immersion into my new life in Tanzania felt like an evolutionary process that, in retrospect, was quite the contrary. It, as I would come to learn, was actually quite dramatic and revolutionary.

As I stood in the crowd with my enormous amount of luggage that warm August night after clearing immigration and customs, I noticed a man holding a sign with the name of the NGO. I had never seen him before, but I could tell by the look on his face that he knew me. Of course he knew me. He had seen a copy of my passport. He greeted me with the first Swahili words spoken to me: "*Karibu* Tanzania."

"*As-salaam Alaikum*," I said. He seemed relieved.

"*Wa alaikum as salaam*," he replied. I am sure he rarely picked up an international visitor that greeted him with the Muslim greeting of peace. I imagined there were few Black Muslim female expats living in Tanzania.

He helped me exchange my currency and warned me not to exchange too much. I only knew this man for minutes, but somehow I instantly trusted him. He loaded up my seven bags of checked luggage, which I now know was ridiculous, with no trepidation. We walked to the car and I stood on the right side. In an unemotional voice, he asked if I was driving. Puzzled, I looked at him, wondering why he'd ask such a thing. Turns out, the right side was the driver's side, not the passenger side as in America. In all my research on Tanzania, I never stumbled across that fact. How embarrassing! I realized I had lots to learn.

CHAPTER 2

THE SOCIAL ORDER

I spent my first night hugging the toilet bowl. It was either a reaction to the anti-malarial meds or the first-class cuisine on one of my lengthy flights. The next morning, I was strong enough to venture out of my hotel by foot for my first full day in Tanzania. I walked along the coast of the Indian Ocean and found myself in the center of the commercial capital of Tanzania. Unfortunately, the day was not as eventful as I imagined. The city center of this usually bustling African city was quite sleepy on the weekend. It was surreal. Here I was in the city center of Tanzania's commercial capital, and like many business centers, people choose to stay away on weekends.

That evening, I ventured out with Tonya, another fellow from my company. Tonya had arrived in Tanzania about one and a half weeks earlier and still was not settled in an apartment. Like many adventurous fellows, the promise of a waiting furnished apartment was broken. She was left to apartment hunt on her own. Tonya took a taxi to my hotel and we headed out to grab a bite to eat. I was glad to meet up with her again. We first met at the training given to all fellows being deployed. We were both Americans, and she lived in New

York City, my birthplace. Tonya was several decades my junior. At least I would have someone else to fill in some of the leisure time after Ramadan. But I assumed that with the generational gap and my adherence to the Islamic faith, the social time we spent together would be limited. Tonya and I did make a connection nevertheless. We were both trying to save the world. Right? I had no idea at the time that she would later be present on one of the most important days of my life.

On my first day I was picked up by one of the organization's drivers. There was no office ready when I arrived. My supervisor let me use a work area that served as a small conference room. But for the most part, like most fellows, we were left to fend for ourselves. My mentor and supervisor told me the first day of my arrival that he planned to go to his homeland in northern Tanzania for two weeks. I was there to make a difference, and everyone assumed I knew what to do. I was to flush out the organization's strategy on reducing the country's maternal mortality rate, write a few project proposals and concept notes. "What is a concept note?" I thought. None of this discouraged me. After all, fellows were partly selected for their ability to work with ambiguity.

On that first day in the office, I met the senior staff. The first thing I noticed was that the most senior of the staff members were not Tanzanian. I later learned that most international NGOs selected country directors that rotate among different countries on a periodic basis. I suspect the thinking was that rotating leaders among different third-world assignments would increase organization cohesiveness and foster a sense of shared vision. A more cynical view would be that those sitting in the head offices in Western countries do not trust the competence or ethics of leaders who come from some of the most corrupt countries of the world. To be fair, most international NGOs attempt to hire locally where possible. However, for many executive positions they find that the candidates do not have the required skills or experience.

As the days went by, I noticed that no one really befriended me. No lunch or dinner invitations, no invitations to visit a home. I found this bizarre. I saw Tonya here and there, but we worked for different NGOs, so our paths didn't cross all that often. My social life was mute.

I ate lunch at the lunch club, which was an outside restaurant within the compound of the office. There was no need to venture out of my cocoon to look for lunch, and no one invited me to do so. For the equivalent of $2, I could get rice, beans, a piece of fruit, and the meat or fish of the day. There was no menu. All food was cooked on the premises in an outside kitchen.

I started the fasting month of Ramadan exactly one week after my arrival. The usual delivery of coffee and tea to the offices of Muslims stopped automatically. The lunch club was only half full. Unlike in the U.S., I was happy not to have to explain to my coworkers why I was not eating. That is one of the reasons I chose Tanzania.

Saidi, the logistic and transport officer who picked me up at the airport, made sure I got settled in my apartment. My use of the organization's car and driver ended after one week. However, Saidi also found someone to transport me by car to and from work. I was treated with privilege, a Black *mzungu*.

My modest, fully furnished, two-bedroom apartment was in the Oyster Bay section of the city. Very few Tanzanians live in Oyster Bay, but they work there as gardeners, security guards and maids. My rent was more than $2,000 plus a $295 service fee, which included electricity, internet, satellite TV, air conditioning, a hot water heater and even a maid. For $7 a week, the maid hand washed my laundry each day. By the time I arrived home from work, my laundry was ironed and folded.

Back in the states, going to the mosque during Ramadan, at least on weekends, was a routine that was as natural as breathing. I assumed it would be the same in Tanzania, especially considering the large Muslim population. However, finding a mosque to pray *tawaweer* was not an easy task. I asked my Muslim coworkers of nearby mosques, but they seemed stumped. I was equally stumped on why they were stumped. After all, many of the Muslim Tanzanian coworkers usually went together to the Friday afternoon prayers at a nearby mosque, but where could they send a *mzungu* Muslim woman alone during the late night? I began to realize that my Muslim coworkers didn't know where to send me because they did not live near the city center or the expat community of Oyster Bay.

"Where can I go for prayers after breaking my fast?" I inquired. I continued, "Back in the States it is the best time of year, I try to go every night but usually at least on weekends. In my mosque back home, we have a big community *iftar* [the meal for breaking the fast]," I explained. "Do you do that here?"

Saidi looked puzzled. "I will get back to you," he replied.

Later that day he told me that my driver, Sadiq, would pick me up from my apartment and take me to a mosque. He would wait for me and return me back to my cocoon in Oyster Bay.

The first night, Sadiq picked me up and took me to a beautiful mosque in city center. I soon realized why he took me to that mosque: everyone spoke English. I also noticed that the only Black and indigenous Tanzanians were the ones cleaning the mosque; the patrons were all East Indian. I was greeted by some women who took me to an area where groups were studying the Quran. It was a spacious mosque with multiple rooms for various activities, but there were no *tawaweer* prayers. That was why I came. I saw a room of women reading duas (prayers). Finally I asked, "What about *tawaweer* [congregational] prayers?"

"This is a Shia mosque, and we do not pray *tawaweer*," I was told. In my 22-years as a Muslim, this was the first I had heard that. I thanked my hostess and keepers of Allah's (*swt*) house. They invited me back, and I returned to my apartment. When I returned to my apartment I realized that to the driver I was *mzungu*, so I was taken not to a place that met my requirements, but to a place where a *mzun-gu* would best fit.

I was not deterred. Sadiq found another mosque to take me, this time in a local area. It was in a residential neighborhood occupied by Black Tanzanians. It obviously did not have the huge financial support like the other. No one greeted me as a newcomer, but they prayed *tawaweer* and that was fine. But unlike the *tawaweer* I had been accustomed to, where a different *iyat* (verse) of the Quran was read with each subsequent *rakat* (prostration unit), the *imam* (leader of the prayer) briskly and repeatedly read the same short *surah* (chapter): Surah Iklas. I realized my knowledge of Islam was limited and felt guilty that I sensed a feeling of unfulfillment for not hearing more quranic verses in the recitation. Sadiq returned me home and I paid him the equivalent of $6.25.

I abandoned the search for the perfect mosque after that. Sadiq's motive was purely economic, and the daily $6.25 for an entire month was out of my personal budget. I became slightly disappointed that in a city that was more than 50% Muslim, I could not find a community to call home during this most holy month. I was also disappointed that my Muslim driver did not think that he would get some reward from the Almighty for taking me to the mosque for my prayers. I continued my daily five required prayers and abandoned the optional *tawaweer*.

As is the case for all organized religions, people adhere to the faith differently, so I noticed differences in Islamic practice. For example, when Ramadan began, the women in the office began wearing the *hijab*, women's head covering. I gave them encouragement as I would expect any Muslim sister would say to another, "You look nice in your *hijab*." I mentioned to Saidi, "I saw that several women in the office had begun wearing *hijab* at work; but, now they stopped." Saidi explained that they only wore for Ramadan. I never made the correlation to Ramadan. I was naive to think that they had an awakening, only to see that they removed it after Ramadan was over. This was strange to me.

--

When I first started my new position, I did not realize that most local staff in the office left their homes at 5:30 AM from the outskirts of the city to arrive at the office by 8:00 AM. They took the *daladala*. It serves as the country's public transport system, but they are usually privately owned. The vehicles can be vans or small buses. Think of rude taxi drivers competing for customers and trying to pack as many people in to maximize profit; that is the *daladala*. The locals rushed to work because they knew they would be shamed if they were late.

It did not take long to realize there were different practices between international and local staff. On business trips, international staff stayed in hotels fit for a Western tourist. I wondered after being dropped off at my hotel, where did all the local staff stay? Unlike international staff who could absorb the cost of *mzungu* accommodations with their per diems and salaries, local staff tried to maximize their daily per diem, or allowance, by staying at local guest houses at a much lower cost and quality. As a visiting American fellow, I was not on a per diem; but, everyone assumed that I should stay at the pricier accommodations. I fell in the category of international staff and felt uncomfortable. I did not want to be privileged. I wanted to connect to my distant cousins. After all, didn't we have similar DNA?

I never asked anyone to introduce me to the life of indigenous Tanzanians. I was curious but still observing the cultural protocols. The only one who reluctantly introduced me to the life of an indigenous Tanzanian was the first person I met in Tanzania, Saidi, the logistics and transport officer I say "reluctant" because I can sum up Saidi's job description as serving the international staff but not to form personal relationships. How could two people of different educational backgrounds, nationalities and workplace statuses connect? It was risky for Saidi to make a first move only to find that the person on the receiving end would yell foul. I slowly began to realize that.

I treated and talked to Saidi like all adults should: as my equal, as my brother in Islam, and considered him my confidant. So when I received an invitation to Thanksgiving dinner by the American country director, I did not hesitate to invite Saidi. After all, the director said to bring a guest. Suspecting that it would upset the social order, I gave my host a heads-up. A few days later, he came to my office for a visit, which was not on his way to any common areas (the lunch club, the bathrooms, the gate or the conference room). It was obvious he had gone out of his way to talk to me.

"How is the project going?" he asked.

I gave him a brief update.

I was surprised by that inquiry since there were about two layers of management reporting between us. Tanzania does not embrace a flat organizational structure; there is a rigid chain of command that must be adhered to. My host organization was no exception.

"You mentioned that you want to bring Saidi to the Thanksgiving dinner," he continued. "You know senior staff will be there?"

I did not know how to reply. I wanted to say, "So, what?" but I bit my tongue and instead said, "You said to bring a guest."

He replied, "I thought you would bring Tonya."

It never crossed my mind that Tonya would be my guest. I had not seen her in weeks. She was a socially conscious young woman who became my friend due to our both being selected as fellows. We were two *mzungus* trying to immerse ourselves in the country, albeit in different ways. We were associates, but we had built different lives in Tanzania.

I realized at that time that I had broken an unspoken taboo, but I did not care. After I politely made it clear that I still had every intention of bringing Saidi, my unexpected visitor knew the conversation was over.

Just as I had planned, Saidi and I both attended the Thanksgiving dinner. No Tanzanian management team attended even though they were invited. Aisha, a fourth generation East Indian Tanzanian project manager, attended with her husband. Everyone was polite, and the assistant country director, a native of Nepal, tried to make Saidi feel comfortable.

There were other *mzungus* from other international NGOs. Overall, it went well and the talk was pleasant enough. Saidi commented quietly to me that all the Tanzanian management team had made excuses not to attend. I naively thought he was overreaching. Maybe it was just a matter of economics and convenience because they did live far.

When it was time to leave, our hostess, the wife of the country director, escorted her departing guests to the door. "Saidi, I do not have a fire extinguisher in my car, and I need that corrected," she said. I was disgusted. It was not the tone of her voice and it was probably for her just an opportune moment to ask. But to me, it felt like a not-so-subtle way of reminding Saidi of his place. That ruined what had been a pleasant evening for both of us. No wonder everyone else made excuses not to come.

CHAPTER 3

TYING THE KNOT

There were several things that attracted me to Saidi. I observed how his peers, superiors and subordinates respected and trusted him. He displayed tenacity in the workplace, constantly striving to meet the expectations set by his superiors. He often used his own personal resources to do what sometimes seemed impossible. Though his efforts frequently went unrecognized, he didn't seem to care. It was all about getting the job done and making others' jobs easier. Yet, more than anything, it was our shared vision of service that led to an unspoken bond.

Saidi introduced me to Tanzanian village life and the people who were previously just statistics to me. Sometimes I accompanied Saidi on work errands. During these short excursions I would see mud thatched roofed houses and often stopped to chat to ask questions to quench my curiosity.

"Where do you get your water?"

"Where did you birth your children?"

"What do you farm?"

"How do you use that utensil? Can you show me?"

"Did you finish primary school?"

It didn't take long for me to realize that philanthropy and giving back was in both of our natures. This man appeared to approach life with integrity and without regard to personal gain. Saidi was quite candid with me about his place in Tanzanian society: a man born in a rural village with only a primary school education, making a salary that I made in high school. I loved his transparency; there was no pretense.

By the time someone is in their 50's, they have a story to tell. Saidi had his and I had mine. We were both ready to write a new chapter— together. Saidi and I seemed to complement each other perfectly. Without him, I would have spent my first six months simply going back and forth between the office and my gated apartment in Oyster Bay. He showed me the real life of the average Tanzanian.

I met Saidi one week before the start of the Muslim holy month of *Ramadan*. Not only do Muslims fast from dawn to sunset, but it is also a time of heightened worship and almsgiving. It was during this time that I saw Saidi for who he really is. I observed how generous he is, digging into his nearly empty pockets to give what little he had.

Because we both did what we could to help those around us, it did not take long for Saidi and me to take on joint philanthropic projects. He helped me find target recipients for the charity that came rolling in from friends and colleagues back home.

Though we are so compatible, it seems our first 50 years of life were worlds apart. Saidi was born in a mud-walled, grass-roofed house just meters from what I call home today. He didn't have his first pair of shoes until the age of ten.

Halfway around the world, I shared my room in the Dyckman projects with my brother. My mom would take me to Buster Brown's to get a new pair of shoes at the start of each school year. Six months later, I would get new patent leathers for Easter.

While Saidi convinced his parents to let him attend a new government elementary school in an adjacent village, I followed my brother and attended the private parochial school St. Matthew Lutheran School.

Both of our young lives were disrupted in the middle of our elementary school education. My mom died when I was eight years old. Within a year, we had to leave the only home I knew. Similarly, Saidi's father died when he was 10; he left his home within 40 days. Despite this disruption, I finished St. Matthew and went on to the acclaimed Bronx High School of Science. Saidi moved in with an uncle and finished his primary education in Mchinga. In 1973, he passed the national exams, but no one who should pay would pay his $3 school fee and $.01 monthly transport cost, so his formal education ends there. Their younger brother's education was not a priority.

Like many rural young men, Saidi ended up in Dar. He went on to get a professional driver's license. One of his first jobs was taking tourists to game reserve parks. Being around so many tourists, he picked up English by ear. He eventually landed a job at an international NGO, gaining more and more responsibility over the 13 years he worked there.

Have you ever tried to complete a 1000-piece puzzle only to discover there was one piece missing? That's how I felt. As a divorced empty nester, I had resigned myself to the thought that 999 would have to do. I knew Saidi felt the same. Being practicing Muslims and socially conservative, a long courtship and dating was out of the question. However, I felt that marrying Saidi would be like finding that missing piece.

I truly admired Saidi, but experience taught me to trust but verify. I knew I needed to ask around to see how others felt about him. About a month before the wedding, I had a week-long program meeting with Margaret, a good friend I had met through Saidi. He always spoke so highly of her, so I thought she would be the right one to help me validate my decision. During one of our breaks, I pulled Margaret aside.

"So Margaret, you are a friend of Saidi and a woman. Should I have any concerns about marrying Saidi?" I asked.

Margaret did not hesitate. "You will get no better than Saidi as a husband."

I felt comfortable sharing more information so I shared, "We decided to move to his homeland in Lindi, in the village."

Margaret had a concerned look on her face. "Don't do it. The family will consume all of his time and resources."

I knew that was a very real possibility, but the move still felt right. I decided to get one more opinion on Saidi. This time, I asked Aisha, the East Indian Tanzanian who was also at the program meeting. I thought it was a good idea to talk to someone who wasn't one of his close friends.

"Guess what," I said. "I am going to get married. I found someone here in Tanzania."

Aisha tried to guess but couldn't. Being a Tanzanian of Indian decent, she was still on the fringe of the inner circle. "Who", she asked.

Not wanting to take any chances, I whispered his name and showed her some pictures on my digital camera.

Aisha gave her classic big smile and hugged me. "That is great!" she said.

Saidi and I married four and a half months after he picked me up from the airport. Prophet Mohamed (*pbuh*) said that when a person gets married, he has completed half of his religion. On that steamy December day, I completed mine. We had a small Muslim ceremony in my apartment in Oyster Bay. In attendance were local staff (including Aisha); Tonya; Sadiq, my driver; Saidi's youngest sister; two of Saidi's senior cousins; the Tanzanian caterers that are used for all-day office meetings with *mzungu* attendees; and Ziyadah, one of my best friends from the States who had arrived in Tanzania the evening before. International staff must have wondered where all their professional Muslim local staff and Margaret went that Friday afternoon.

Because of all the unwritten rules regarding international and local staff, I didn't inform many people that Saidi and I were getting married. However, as time went by, some grew suspicious because Saidi would often check up on me in my office and replaced Sadiq as my regular driver. Frequently, as he was seen leaving my office, a co-worker would wave her finger and say with a big grin, "Something is wrong here." Saidi would just chuckle and keep walking.

Our measured silence was solely to protect Saidi's job and to avoid speculation about where we would be living. Local staff often protected each other if it did not jeopardize their own position, but still rumors spread. Saidi would sometimes tell me the "radio wood" was active, the term used for the rumor mill. Apparently though, radio wood was only active among the local staff. Weeks after the locals knew, the international staff was shocked to hear of our marriage. It indicated to me how big the social divide was. When Saidi told his country director of our marriage, all he had to say was, "Good luck." To be certain, we were breaking a taboo, but that was none of our concern. Fortunately, I did not have the same trepidation with my co-workers back home. I knew I would tell them during our next video conference.

Tonya knew the secret before anyone else. She left work and came over to my apartment for the wedding. She draped a *kanga* over her head, respecting the Muslim tradition, and did a fabulous job ensuring that my family in the States saw the wedding live via Skype.

Khalid was my *wali* for the wedding. A *wali* is a Muslim bride's male representative. The closest analogy to a Christian wedding is that Khalid gave me away. Khalid was a mature, professional young Muslim brother, a real family man. Saidi and I knew Khalid from the office.

Months earlier, he invited me to spend *Eid-ul-fitr*, the festival celebrating the end of the fasting month of Ramadan, with his family on the island of Zanzibar. You can reach Zanzibar by ferry in 70 minutes or 20 minutes by airplane. Not wanting to impose, I reluctantly declined his heartfelt invitation. Because Ramadan is either 29 or 30 days based on the moon sighting, there was a chance I would have to be a house guest for two days. I did not want to impose more than a day in a house I had never visited before. So I hesitantly declined his offer to spend my Eid on Zanzibar, an island with a rich Muslim history that is still more than 90% Muslim.

I was unsure of where our relationship stood after I declined his offer, so you can imagine my delight when he accepted my request to be my *wali*. Years later, we still correspond. I even call him my father. It doesn't matter that he is my junior.

Aisha brought the incense to the wedding. We worked closely together in the office. She taught me a lot about a world I was unfamiliar with, the NGO world. Like most East Indian Tanzanian Muslims I had met, Aisha was Shia. And like most young Tanzanians of Indian ancestry, she was educated in the West due to the relative wealth of her parents and grandparents. Her husband did not attend, because it was Ashura, a Shia holiday. With it being a sacred time for Shia Muslims, I was honored by her presence and thoughtfulness. She scented my honeymoon clothes with the smoke from burning incense. She explained that smell was an aphrodisiac and assured me it would last. I thought that it was a nice smell but our "honeymoon" was going to be a road trip to Serengeti, Ngorongoro Crater, and Kilimanjaro with my friend Ziyadah.

This pleasant assembly of unlikely people in my apartment in Oyster Bay confirmed where I best fit. Yet, it was not a perfect fit. I resented the previous warnings and sometimes not-so-subtle looks of disappointment disguised as well-meaning advice from international staff. My resentment eventually withered and so did theirs. After all, it was only Dar. It was not yet the bush, where I would find myself even more of a cultural outsider.

John Grey, the author of Men Are from Mars, Women Are from Venus asserts that women need to feel loved and men need to feel appreciated. I agree with him. Not a day goes by that I do not feel loved by my husband, and I make every effort to show him constant appreciation. Saidi also makes every effort to show he loves me. Yes, it took 5 years for him to learn how to make me coffee but if I am stressed, he is stressed. He often says, "I brought you here to the bush and I am responsible. Your father told me to take care of you and I promised him I will." For my part, every time we get a flat tire, every time the generator won't start, every time he must protect us from some predator, and every time he brings that morning coffee, I say *"pole"* and then "thank you" the best way I can.

CHAPTER 4

THE HOMELAND

Though I came into my fellowship with no expectations, moving and starting a new life still required a bit of adjustment. I had to quit my job, but that was eased by the generous severance pay. To further ease my transition, Saidi gave me a choice of where to live. I felt like the wife from the American sitcom Green Acres. Would it be the city of Dar es Salaam, the suburbs of Dar es Salaam or the rural countryside of the bush? I wasn't sure yet where I would be most comfortable.

One weekend, Saidi and I snuck off to the village of Ruvu, his homeland, located in Tanzania's Lindi region on the coast of the Indian Ocean in Southeast Tanzania. The term "homeland" is often used by Tanzanians to refer to their ancestral lands. Ruvu village has less than 100 homes. Its population is barely 500. Some say it is too small to be a village and for many years it was not a village, in the government records anyway. It lost its village designation when the government decided it was too small to manage and it was placed under Mchinga 2. This meant that all government and private projects were managed from Mchinga. Ruvu residents felt that they were being shortchanged on development projects and aid. However, in 2012, after much complaining, they were finally given the designation of an official independent village.

Travel weary, Saidi decided to break the trip up. After driving for six long hours, we passed the junction to Ruvu and continued 30 minutes to the nearest town. Lindi town is within Lindi district, which is within one of the over 20 regions of Tanzania. Lindi district has no industry, but old abandon railroad tracks, ports, and buildings are reminders of its more prosperous colonial past.

The next day, we got up and continued on to the fishing village of Ruvu. It is difficult to describe the location of Ruvu without describing the two Mchinga villages you must pass. Saidi is a son of Mchinga. He attended his last few years of primary school there. When we tell people we live in Ruvu, people get confused, but when we tell them we live near Mchinga, they say things like, "Oh, I pass Mchinga on the road going to Dar."

Mchinga 1 is located on the main paved road, and Mchinga 2 is located a small distance from the paved road. Due in large part to their locations, both Mchingas have access to fresh water and more services than Ruvu. Mchinga 1 has a dispensary, or small medical clinic, and is busy with buses and trucks. Mchinga 2 has a secondary school. Unlike Ruvu and its other adjacent villages, the Mchingas are on the grid. I figured I would have no problem blending in places as busy as the Mchingas. I soon found I was sadly mistaken.

To reach Ruvu from Mchinga, you must navigate 18-kilometer of rough road. We arrived with a car full of rice. Saidi had planned a charity dinner for the village. He bought fresh fish to go with it. After my first night hugging the porcelain bowl, I knew not to take chances with my stomach. I was suspicious of village sanitation protocol. No fresh fish for me that night. I ate from my survival kit: canned tuna, crackers and breakfast bars.

As we entered the village, all eyes were on us—and by "us," I mean our car. Cars are a big deal in Ruvu, so the children started jumping up and down yelling, "*gari, gari, gari,*" meaning "car, car, car." I felt an immediate invasion of privacy as people crowded around us. Saidi opened the back door, and villagers immediately began to help unload the rice. The children peeked into the windows to get a glimpse of the dashboard and our cargo. I noticed they were all thin, so very thin.

We slept in what seemed to be one of the best homes in Ruvu. It belonged to the *imam* (the Muslim cleric) of Ruvu, a friend of Saidi's. It had cement walls, a corrugated metal sheet roof and a toilet— one of the only ones in the village. That last feature earned it the privilege of hosting the First Lady of Tanzania when she visited Ruvu for a funeral.

I stayed in our room while Saidi coordinated the charity dinner his niece cooked at her house nearby. I stayed alone with my thoughts as Saidi attended to the village dinner. After he returned, we took a late night walk to see the mosque and Islamic school that would later become the center of much of our philanthropic work over the following year. Later that night, despite the usual disruptions of a middle-aged bladder, I slept peacefully with the starlit sky in view. The cool breeze was magnificent.

After my very safe and conservative meal of tuna and crackers early the next morning, Saidi's niece and a nephew escorted us to Jome (pronounced Joe-may). Jome is considered part of Ruvu and is the actual place of Saidi's birth. To get there, you must abandon your car, take a dhow (small boat) across the river, walk over a bed of rocks, go past the mangrove forest and finally walk the last 45 minutes of the way. It is not a trip for the faint hearted. The place is so remote that I didn't see even one person the whole way there. Elders often remarked that it had been years since they last visited. With age, the trip becomes too strenuous.

Once there, Saidi insisted on swimming in the ocean, so while his niece and nephew waited, we went to the far side of the beach and had our own private swim party. A wave of happiness, nostalgia and peace seemed to overcome Saidi. After all, his family had left this place in 1968. Finally, he had returned.

It was then that it hit me. I thought, "New York City, done that. Suburbia, did that. Expensive and congested Dar es Salaam? NOT." Jome enveloped me. It had a magical way of making this *mzungu* feel at home. I decided we would build right there. Saidi was delighted.

I was not the first *mzungu* in Ruvu. The Germans had been there, too, and some decades ago it had been a port city. In fact, as you walk through the bush, you can still find an old railroad track that was used for transporting sisal (a plant of many uses). You can also see the ruins of the old dock when traveling between Ruvu and Jome.

Bint Masud, an elderly woman I met on my first trip, asked in Swahili, "She is going to live here?" Then she answered her own question. "Well, *mzungu*s love the beach." Years later, I would rate Bint Masud one of the wisest people I have ever met.

Even after a year of traveling between Lindi town and Ruvu, people of Mchinga still gawked at me. And I too made many observations. I noticed the men sat around, playing a local board game. It reminded me of seniors playing dominoes on the boardwalk of Coney Island. Saidi would jokingly call it the jobless area. It is true. I always wondered, with no visible industry or offices, how do people earn their income?

Saidi often stopped the car to give his *salaams* (greetings) to the *wazee* (elders). I hated when the car stopped. With Saidi often engaged in a conversation with an old schoolmate, young children would come to my side of the car and gawk unapologetically. Coming from New York City, where someone could walk through the subway cars naked and not be noticed, I felt panic and extreme anxiety from this unwelcomed attention. I asked Saidi what I could say when people stare. He taught me, "*Nina mavi usoni?*" or "Do I have poo on my face?" I used it a few times with childish delight.

Soon however, I came to realize I needed to understand from the locals' perspective. I was a curiosity. Shoot, all vehicles were a curiosity. Still, I continued to feel insulted and offended when I heard people calling me "*mzungu*." I knew that if the children called me that, the adults had to as well. Who could believe a 5-year-old White child calling an African American "ni....r" without it being taught in that child's home?

In the early days, I used to buy candy and bring it to the villages we would visit. I had quite a following as children began to anticipate the candy. I would hear them say, "*pipi*" (pee-pee), a Swahili word for candy, and put out their little soiled hands. I began to dislike this ritual for many reasons. First, I felt I was promoting a culture of begging that was so prominent on the corners of Dar. Second, even with parents looking on, few thanked me. The children began to track me down from their homes in their soiled, torn play clothes. They would come back for seconds and thirds. Saidi blamed me for starting something he knew would get out of hand. This ritual ended permanently with the utterance of one word from a child's mouth: *mzungu*.

I am still called a *mzungu*, but I do not really consider it an insult anymore. I figure it is a term of reference, kind of like referring to someone as "the tall guy next door." People continue to use the term when looking for directions to Jome: "It is where the Tanzanian lives who is married to a *mzungu*."

How someone perceives a potentially derogatory term depends on the context. I can say it: "Just ask for the house where the *mzungu* lives." But when children in Ruvu surrounded the car after several years of living in the bush and sang, "Mama *Mzungu*, Mama *Mzungu*, Mama *Mzungu*," my eyes welled up. I was shook. It felt like they were saying, "You are an outsider, and you always will be."

I thought, I am a Black woman returning to the continent that her ancestors were ripped from more than three centuries earlier. Yes, I understood that my skin was lighter than theirs, just like many other African Americans whose female ancestors hosted unwanted visits from their slave owners. Yes, I had accepted that language would always be a barrier. However, I could not understand how parents could look on as their children taunted me. A familiar sick feeling came over me. It was déjà vu.

It was the same feeling that overcame me more than two decades earlier as I pushed my daughter in a stroller in Portage, Michigan. Passengers from a speeding car yelled out the window, "Go back to where you came from!" Where, back to New York? Or, did they mean back to Africa? Unlikely. It was during America's Desert Storm military operation. I understood what those passersby meant; they meant to anywhere but America. And, just like two decades earlier, I was not going anywhere. Slowly, I began to realize that I would always be a *mzungu*. Over time, I learned that it is all about the context that determines if and how much offense should be taken. Nevertheless, my visits to Ruvu became less frequent. Yet, I had come to accept that Ruvu was my village. It was my new address. It was hard to believe that a few years earlier I had just set foot in this country.

When I arrived in Tanzania to begin my six-month fellowship, I was months away from receiving my PhD. I had locked up my 3,600-square foot home and new car. I will return, I thought. Shortly after arriving in Tanzania though, I was ready to let it all go. My employer had trained us for re-entry. At the time, none of us knew I would never re-enter.

About a year after my arrival in Tanzania, I was asked by a friend to reach out to another fellow alumnus that was having trouble with re-entry back into the United States after a similar deployment. It is common for fellows to have a difficult transition back to their previous lives after experiencing such a rich experience in remote regions of Africa, Asia or South America.

How do you prepare a 30-second answer to the water cooler question, "How did it go?" How do you feel when you see people's eyes glaze over with boredom when you tell them how it really was? How do you respond when someone changes the subject to the inconveniences of their life: the nanny showed up late, the car did not start, the boat needs to be stored for the winter.

I gave some advice via email, but I never heard back. Maybe I gave bad advice, or maybe, being a Black *mzungu*, my advice was not applicable to a White *mzungu*. Or, more than likely, she realized that this *mzungu* was like her, but I was not returning.

CHAPTER 5

UNEXPECTED MZUNGU GUESTS

Because Jome is a beautiful and remote place located on a beach, sometimes visitors wander onto our land. Our first unexpected guests were two adventurous couples: one Australian and one Dutch. We were not home as our house was under construction and we were renting a house 50 km away in Lindi town. The construction workers were the only ones there to greet the surprise visitors. When we called to inquire on the building progress, we were informed of our *mzungu* visitors.

Upon hearing that we had outsiders at the site, a maternal instinct took over. I felt protective of the fishermen and others that get their livelihood from the ocean near Jome. Recently, there had been land speculation in nearby villages. I was cautious. I spoke to the Dutch gentleman on the phone, and he offered to leave. I invited them to stay the night and told him we would see them in the morning.

Upon arriving in Jome, it became apparent they were harmless and really tourists. The two couples had solar-powered, self-contained vehicles that were equipped with a bathroom and a kitchen. They had setup camp 75-kilometers from our building site. I actually enjoyed our visitors, so I invited them to stay a second night.

The two couples met in Mali and came to Tanzania together. The Dutch couple drove their vehicle from Holland and had been on the road exploring Africa for two months. They were following an old German map that had Ruvu listed. The couples figured our village of Ruvu could provide a scenic oceanfront campsite. I believe the Australian couple started in South Africa.

They were truly adventurous, experienced travelers who were enjoying what Africa had to offer. The Dutch couple had already travelled in West Africa. They were now heading north towards Sudan. They were a nice break for me. I finally had some folks to chat with.

CHAPTER 6

THE LANGUAGE OF THE LAND

Thanks to Disney, most Americans know a few words of Swahili without realizing it. Though popular, *Hakuna matata*, meaning "no worries," is not really used in daily conversation. Simba is not only the name of a darling cartoon lion but is the actual word for lion. These words are a safe bet. But thinking you know a little Swahili can get you in trouble.

Take the words for wood, mosquito and the male genital organ. I learned early on that if you did not speak perfect Swahili, stay away from the words *mbao*, *mbu*, and *mboo*. "There are many *mbu*," or is it, "There are many *mboo*"? The latter is the male genital organ and the former is a mosquito.

I remember once making a grossly embarrassing linguistic mistake in a store. I confused the word for the number ten (*kumi*) with the word for a female genital part (*kuma*). Close enough, I thought as I struggled for the right words but I was so glad the shopkeeper was female.

I blamed my lack of knowledge of Swahili on my mature age, but there was one other *mzungu*, Nancy, an Asian expat, who really made me realize just how slowly I was picking up Swahili. She had been in the country about the same length of time as me. I have always been a little envious of people who can easily pick up a language, and Nancy was picking it up like fire. She was a young Korean-American who, partly due to the dismal job market back in the States and partly due to her naturally adventurous nature, decided to volunteer in Tanzania with the hope of more substantial employment. While I could barely pronounce the name of the local neighborhoods, Nancy was effortlessly taking the *daladala* back and forth to the office. She had adapted to the life that most Tanzanian's live, even taking her daily baths from a plastic bucket. I admired her carefree nature and her ease of immersing herself into the Tanzanian society.

Occasionally, Saidi and I offered Nancy a ride home. The two of them would converse effortlessly, throwing in a Swahili word now and then. Realizing I was sometimes lost in the conversation, Saidi would sometimes translate for me the missing link. I was still struggling with "good morning." But when she said, "*shikamoo*," and Saidi gave the typical reply, "*marahaba*," I knew she had succeeded in doing what I had not.

Shikamoo and *marahaba* are words whose nuanced meaning can't be translated. To me, *Shikamoo* symbolized acceptance and respect. Young children say it to elders as they pass by. Children say it to their parents or grandparents. The confusing thing is that it is not only a matter of age that determines who says it to whom. One must also consider where you fall on the family tree.

Saidi, being the 17th of his father's 21 children, has many nieces, nephews, great-nieces, and great-nephews who are decades older than him. Still, people say it to Saidi and me because I am his wife. For example, when a group of extended family members meet, it is an interesting scene to hear the flurry of *shikamoos* and *marahabas* based not on age, but on birth position. I have learned to quietly ask Saidi when it is appropriate to say it. In other words, I ask if the very old person in front of me is my elder or if I am his or hers.

Though Nancy greeted Saidi with the respectful term, she never greeted me the same way. I thought it was odd, especially since I'm older than Saidi so I asked her why. She said it was because we were friends. That was a new explanation for me but I liked it. Even among native Tanzanians, Saidi was usually appropriately greeted with *shikamoo* from those his junior, but I was not. I began to wonder if I was not worthy of this respectful greeting given to those who are your senior. When Saidi would tell tongue-tied young natives to greet me with it, they would say, "Oh, we did not know she knew Swahili." They were always tickled when I replied, *"Marahaba."*

Those with a moderate level of education and any knowledge of English did not like to use the greeting with me. Rather, they would practice their English. With time, I became comfortable practicing the little bit of Swahili I knew.

As a non-native speaker, *shikamoo* wasn't the only thing I struggled with. For instance, the double consonant at the beginning of Swahili words drove me crazy. A word beginning with the letters m and n and followed by a consonant may incorrectly be pronounced as an entire syllable. You know someone's new to the language if they say, "I am travelling to the southern city Ma-twa-ra." No, it is Mtwa-ra, the southern city of Mtwara. Also troubling is the word *ngombe* or cow. It is not na-gom-be. It is ngom-be. But even more challenging is the pig-like sound you have to make when saying it.

I was tickled to see that I was not the only one struggling with this double consonant problem. The assistant country director during my fellowship pronounced my supervisor's name Na-daki. Because he is a *mzungu*, no one corrected him. It is spelled Ndaki, pronounced Nda-ki. In case you wondering, it is not ma-zun-gu.

Sometimes the extra syllables make all the difference. If you want to tell someone to go slowly, you say, *"Pole pole"* (poe-lay-poe-lay), meaning "Take it slowly." If you get lazy and only say *pole*, then you are saying "so sorry." *Pili* could be the name of a woman, maybe a waitress. But say it twice in a restaurant, *pilipili*, and someone will bring you hot peppers.

I often wondered why syllables need to be said twice to convey a concept. Like the word *daladala* for local transport buses or vans. Why not just dala? And not to be outdone by the mass transit *daladala*, a motorcycle is not a pike, but a *pikepike*. In my village, instead of using the Swahili word for butterfly, *kipepeo*, they say *kiputepute*. It is not kipute. It is enough to make you *kizunguzungu* (dizzy).

If I had been a better student of Arabic, Swahili would be easier. Approximately one fourth of Swahili words are from the Arabic language, and many Muslims in Tanzania are competent in conversational Arabic. Many Swahili words are variations of Arabic words. It reminds me of how a parent talks to a young child, making words more child friendly.

The letter "i" has been added to many words. For example, the Muslim holiday Eid is pronounced Eid-ie. My husband's name, Saidi, would just be Sayed in Arabic. The Arabic name Sadiq is Sadiqi in Swahili. Mohamed is Mohamedi. However, because of its Arab roots, you can see it written both ways. I was surprised that the common Muslim name of Ali is often written as Ally.

Similarly, when I previously purchased Rosetta Stone to learn Arabic, I often found myself unmotivated to study my Swahili version. I never finished the program. Both times, I reached a plateau and never grew past a few basic phrases.

Later, when the first female school teacher was assigned to my village primary school, I thought it would be a great opportunity to hire a Swahili tutor. During her school break, we met three times a week for about a month. It was better, but I noticed I was just memorizing sentences like a tourist. She found it difficult to explain when to say zote instead of wote or chote. She could not teach the rules. When she travelled elsewhere to finish out her school break, I never resumed the lessons. Later, I found out that private teaching colleges are the primary path for students who fail secondary school. She was no exception. Crazy, right?

After moving to Tanzania, I had to revise my definition of what a college is. Anyone with the financial means, regardless of academic performance in the government secondary schools, can be accepted into any of the country's so-called private colleges. My language teacher was no exception. And that year, sadly, not one of Ruvu's primary school students passed the national exam to advance to secondary school.

Another *mzungu* recommended a Swahili learning book. It turned out to be the best Swahili language book for *mzungus* I ever had. In ten lessons, it explained the rules. I was riveted by the book. It gave me the confidence I was previously lacking. But a book designed for Kenyan or Tanzanian Swahili will not explain what *kiputiputi* means.

Each area has its dialect, and a Tanzanian can tell from which area or tribe someone comes by their pronunciation or even by his or her name.

It is the same back in the States. Despite three decades of living in Middle America, most Americans can tell I am from the Northeast but not quite a New Englander. I remember my first visit to Rhode Island when people looked at me strange when I asked for a soda. "Soda? You mean 'pop'?" they'd say. Pop was what we called my grandfather; it was not a soft drink.

Because they are taught the British dialect, even those Tanzanians who speak English often have trouble understanding me. Saidi says I speak "strong English," whatever that means. I thought about my first experience with British English on the island nation of Malta. I ordered a coffee with cream. Makes sense, I thought. The waiter frowned and put whip cream on my coffee. I ordered lemonade and he brought a lemon-lime soft drink.

Since then, I have learned that an elevator is a lift, and a paved road is a tarmac. The car's windshield is the windscreen, and a flat tire is a puncture. A cellphone is always a mobile, not a mobile phone.

Saidi had no idea what a glove compartment of a car was, maybe because they do not need gloves in this equatorial nation. He simply calls it a drawer.

For the English speaking *mzungu*, Swahili is actually much easier to learn than other foreign languages. If I was younger—my excuse for not learning—it would roll off my tongue. Several modern words have been adapted from English, for example *baiskeli* (bicycle) and *kamati* (committee). Another big plus is that there is no difference in conjugation based on gender.

There is no linguistic distinction between the female and male. Saidi told me, "We are an equal opportunity society." Well, that may be a leap of faith, but I will take it. Of course, that makes the reverse, a native Swahili-speaking person speaking English, more problematic. I am often frustrated by Saidi's careless use of "he" and "she." Who are you talking about, your aunt or uncle? Thankfully the words for "aunt" and "uncle" are different.

My basic phrases do come in handy, however. One day Mwamba, not Ma-wam-ba, an entrepreneur from Ruvu, brought us a red snapper. He owns a small store and has expanded his business to transporting fish from Ruvu to Mchinga thanks to the purchase of a *pikepike*. Mwamba called Saidi's mobile. I decided to take the call since Saidi was outside. Mwamba said that he had fish. Luckily, he is not too shy to try to converse with me even though he does not speak English. In Swahili, I told him to bring the fish. After Saidi returned, I told him of my conversation with Mwamba. He did not believe I communicated correctly and envisioned Mwamba waiting for us to come to Ruvu. Saidi prepared to go to the village to meet Mwamba, but before we could leave, we heard Mwamba's *pikepike* coming. "Ha! I told you I speak Swahili, a little anyway," I gloated.

I was proud when I could make people smile when I reply to inquiries about fish in my village of Ruvu. "Wavuvi Ruvu wavivu," I would say, which means "The fishermen of Ruvu are lazy." Or was it, "The lazy people of Ruvu are fishermen"?

CHAPTER 7

WHAT IS IN A NAME?

Names have meaning. When Muslim women get married, they can keep their family names instead of taking their husband's. Yes, some still decide to take their husband's name, but I consider this a practice adapted from their country's colonial past. Another common practice in the Muslim and Arab world is to take your father's first name as your middle name. Hence, all siblings have the same middle name regardless of gender. Some take it a bit further and add the paternal grandfather's name and his father's. However, the family name is tacked on at the end to tie all the family together. I accepted this naming practice and understood it until I came to Tanzania.

Among the Muslims here, there seems to be no family name to tie a family together. Your middle name is your father's first name and your last name is your grandfather's first name. This means that a father's last name is different from his children's. Yes, children have their father's first name as their middle name, but they have his middle name as their last name. It is all very confusing.

In the village, most women are known as their father's daughters. For example, if a woman's father's name is Abdullah, she is called Bint Abdullah. Bint is both the Arabic and Swahili word for daughter, but in this context, it means "daughter of." It is a good way to preserve the lines of lineage.

One day, Saidi shared with me that his boyhood name was Kombania. He seems proud of that name because of its uniqueness. But he considers it disrespectful if someone his junior uses it. It is the name given to him at birth. It translates to "brigade." However, after his *jando* (circumcision), at the age of seven, he received a new name of his choosing. That's where the name Saidi came from.

To add to the confusion, many people are known by a nickname. The name is based on a habit or event. Saidi's uncle became known as Ngwena after an attack by a crocodile. Ngwena is a local Swahili name for crocodile. (Mamba, not to be confused with mwamba, is the formal name for crocodile.) Ngwena's son, Saidi's cousin, is known as Ali Ngwena. With so many men named Ali, Mohamed, Hassan, Saidi, Hamis, Juma and many other common Muslim names, it is no wonder these nicknames stick.

Saidi and I started giving private names to people based on our own experiences with them. Our second fulltime helper in Jome was also our neighbor. He is known as Bangi, which translates to marijuana. No wonder he was red eyed and sometimes excessively talkative. But I thought it was sad when his young daughter, Zena, made a homemade license plate for her new bicycle that read "Zena Bangi. I tried not to use the name Bangi and called him by what I think is his given name, Mwenda.

Bangi is also called Mr. Gazelle by us because of his gazelle trapping skills. Mr. Stone was the person to cut through the hard stone used to make a hole for our septic system and water cistern. He was later fired, however, because of his involvement in selling our cement during our month long Muslim pilgrimage of hajj. From that point on, he became known as Mr. Thief.

Juma replaced Mr. Thief as the stone digger. He was hard working, but with Juma being such a common name, we called him Juma Choo. We could never call him that to his face though, because choo means toilet. What is a toilet without a septic tank? Juma worked hard manually digging through rock to create our septic and cistern over a six-month period. More on that later.

Mr. Cow lives in Ruvu and is responsible for the management of Ruvu's herd of cows. One late evening, the village heard mooing in the darkness. It was a cow Mr. Cow had tried to sell, without permission, in town. Mr. Cow is not the only self-appointed entrepreneur in my village. There is also Mr. Contractor. He somehow always manages to become the leader of village projects, the road improvement project most notably.

Ruvu received a grant from a local NGO to widen the approach road to its village and move concrete to the road. Villagers were paid by the number of meters they cleared and the number of buckets of concrete they loaded on a hired tipper truck. Predictably, the villagers accused Mr. Contractor of embezzling some of the money. The project stopped for a while until students who needed school fees could be hired with the remaining funds. Saidi and I found ourselves in the same dilemma we tried to avoid: too many people with the name Mr. Thief.

Sijoli, one of Saidi's relatives, worked for us for a while. We initially hired Sijoli to take care of our cows and goats, then just the cows, and finally just the goats. As his responsibilities were reduced, his salary was proportionately reduced until it finally went to zero. Sijoli means "I do not care" in Swahili. Unfortunately, it is a fitting name. Sijoli did not care if our cows needed water. He never reported if an animal was sick. He lived in a local house we built, but when a tree crashed the fence, we had to hire Bangi to cut it down. Sijoli could very well have been called Bangi too, as I believe this is one of the reasons he really did not care.

When Sijoli moved to Jome from the village, he did not have a bed and slept on a cardboard box in a mud house Saidi built years earlier for Sijoli's uncle. Eventually, Saidi let Sijoli sleep in a house we had built for visiting family. He went to war with Sijoli about not even having a bed sheet. Finally, we learned from a village elder that Sijoli's name was really Abdu Rahman, a noble Muslim name. I began calling him Abdu Rahman for a while, thinking that calling him Sijoli was causing a self-fulfilling prophesy.

One day we saw him open our goat *banda* (hut) and let a goat out to graze with something protruding from her rear. We called the doctor, who arrived immediately. He examined the goat and then pulled out a dead fetus. Saidi buried it. Sijoli returned in the evening to lock up the goats and never asked what happen. To this day, he still hasn't been informed of the doctor's visit. I went back to calling him Sijoli.

All of these experiences with workers, friends and family taught me to verify then trust. Saidi seemed to already know that, but even he was often caught off guard. It is here that I learned how adaptation is a lesson in perseverance.

CHAPTER 8

NO WATER, NO LIFE

"Water coming today?" When I was a child in Manhattan, this type of question was unheard of. Water was everywhere! In the summer, we often cooled off under the open fire hydrants and sprinklers in the neighborhood park. Even as an adult in the suburbs of Michigan, spring meant opening and testing the sprinkler system to make sure the lush lawn stayed green throughout the summer. Not watering your grass could have invited the scowls of neighbors. That is the world I came from.

Water was not an issue in the gated communities of Oyster Bay where I lived during my fellowship. Somehow, the landlords shielded their expat guests from the depravity most Tanzanians suffered yet accepted on a daily basis. I began to understand the exorbitant rent and service fees charged by landlords. It costs to keep a fantasy alive.

In Jome, life revolves around the existence or non-existence of water. After three days of trying to get water delivered to our rented house in Lindi town, our water arrived, unpredictable as usual. On our way to visit Jome, we saw women with buckets on Mtanda Hill, our first residence in Lindi. "Water coming today?" Saidi asked. Yep, indeed. Buckets are a priceless commodity in a water-starved nation. In the commercial capital of Dar and a scarcely populated rural village, a plastic bucket is a lifeline.

In addition to the appearance of mud puddles, laundry hanging outside thatch-roofed mud houses is a good indication that it has recently rained. Not wanting to use precious drinking and cooking water, women and children can be seen with buckets and powdered laundry soap, washing anywhere water has gathered. Rivers that were previously dry become bustling with activity. Bare-butt children bathe nearby, undeterred by the women doing the household laundry. Goats and chickens fill their bellies with water, knowing they must take advantage of this gift.

Residents lined up with a stack of empty multicolored, five-gallon pails or anything else they could carry water with. It was easy to spot the business people. They were the ones with carts full of clear and amber 20-liter plastic containers, each with a screw-on plastic lid. A whole economy surrounding water had emerged. This was the case in Dar but not in Oyster Bay.

Water in Tanzania is rationed and sent by the government. And before we left for hajj, we were lucky that our rental house in Lindi had an abundance of water. National elections were coming up and when the president campaigned in Lindi, he stayed a few houses from us. (The first lady is from Lindi and owns a house on the hill.) During this presidential visit, the city kept sending water to Mtanda Hill. It reminded me of a comment made to me in Libya about garbage pickup: "We know when Gaddafi is coming to our neighborhood because the streets are cleaned and garbage is picked up."

Due to the president's presence, our water cistern was overflowing. By the time we left for hajj, the cistern was ¾ full. Why, then, was it only ½ full upon our return? We asked our guard, who admitted that one of our neighbors asked for water because it was not delivered the entire month we were gone. Our neighbor never mentioned it when I visited her upon our return. We questioned our guard again. He said she only came once. I texted my neighbor, just saying I was confirming my guard's story as maybe he was selling water. She came over to the house maybe five minutes later and admitted she took maybe ten buckets (20 liters each) over three consecutive days. It did not add up as maybe 3,000 liters were gone.

Luckily, the city sent another 3,000 liters that night. In all fairness, our neighbors were generous when we first arrived. We had little water, but they had an abundance to share. It did not take long to realize that this was not an isolated incident.

When our car was in the shop for maintenance, it appeared to passersby that we weren't home. As a result, we had an unwanted visitor one morning. "Come, come," I heard Saidi call to me in a quiet voice. A girl had opened our cistern, lowered her bucket and was helping herself to our water. Her excuse: "I knocked on the door to ask, but no one answered." I did not understand her logic. I used one of the few Swahili words I knew, making sure she heard me. "Mwizi," I said firmly, meaning "thief." But what can a thief logically say? Caught red-handed, we told her not to move. Luckily, our neighbor's housekeeper identified her as one of our neighbors. I was more concerned about the safety of our water supply than the thief herself. We immediately had a metal grill made and affixed a padlock. We removed that metal security grill on moving day. It is now in use in Jome.

Our water bill was $8/month, but it was a crap shoot knowing when they would deliver, and our tank was almost empty. We would have to hire a truck to deliver water if the city did not send it soon. With the cement cistern nearly empty, we decided to clean it.

Lindi town was challenging enough, but our focus was on water in Jome. From the first day we decided to make our new life in Lindi district, we strategized on how to get water in Jome. The immediate need was water for building, but our long-term survival depended on our ability to source water permanently. A big part of our daily life was spent addressing our daily water challenges in town and our soon-to-be home in Jome.

The same day we cleaned our cistern in town, we bought a plastic tank to hold water in Jome. Then we had to hire a truck from a mosque to deliver it. Fuel is about twice the cost in Tanzania as it is in the States. I was beginning to learn that our two largest recurring expenses would be fuel and water.

We were among the minority in Tanzania who had indoor plumbing in our rental home. There was no question that our new home would have it too. I was all about the local experience, but running water was a must-have. Although the problem of getting water was still unsolved, we went full steam ahead with our plan to have a house with close-to-first world plumbing.

During the dry season, the land and people begin to long for the rain. Everyone speculates and looks for signs to signal the start of the first rain of the season. So when we heard frogs croaking, the sound of this once-silenced creature was music to our ears. At last, the awful humidity of the previous month had finally come raining down on us in full force. We were getting the long-awaited first torrential rain of the season. There was no wind. Just down pouring rain on and off, mostly on. I could not sleep, because I was visualizing water pouring into our cement water cistern from our roof gutters.

One evening, Saidi mumbled something about his first job in the morning being to pump water from the cistern to the plastic reserve storage tank. I was excited because the cistern was the highest it had ever been, 95% full. And this was only the season of the short rains. I had the urge to wash something. Rain is truly a blessing.

For those of you who, like me four years earlier, use water like it is unlimited, whose water bills are just an annoyance because they are much less than most other recurring expenses, or who are annoyed because there is a ban on sprinkling your plush suburban lawns, this is how it works in Jome and many other homes and offices with plumbing.

We have a 5,000-liter poly tank and a 40,000-liter cement cistern. It took about five months to dig the stony earth by hand. The latter is fed from either a water truck or rain water. The former, the plastic tank, was the only place we had to store water for our first year as we struggled to solve leakage problems from the brick cement-lined cistern.

The house is fed from a 2,000-liter plastic tank that sits on a 20-foot tower; water enters the home's plumbing system by gravity. When we have an abundance of rain, we quickly pump it to the 2,000-liter tank, and then transfer water over to the 5,000-liter poly tank. Why, you may ask? Three reasons: 1) to make room for more rain water in the cement water cistern; 2) to secure at least 5,000 liters in case the cement cistern still has leakage; and 3) to put water in the plastic tank to prevent it from cracking under the equatorial sun.

The importance of gutters becomes evident when it rains. I remember those days of cleaning the gutters in Michigan to prevent ice jams during the winter. There, it was equally important to have gutters to take water away from the foundation of the home to prevent wet basements. Well, in Tanzania, we have no basements and no ice jams, but gutters are still crucial because they're used to capture rain. In the village, if someone is fortunate enough to replace their thatched roof with corrugated metal sheets, they are congratulated for having a more efficient method of capturing this scarce resource. Every roof is looked upon as a potential resource for capturing water.

From our roof, we can harvest enough water for ten days from one hour of seasonal torrential rainfall. I have begun to look at the goat *bandas* and the poultry house as lost opportunities as the water from these structures pours, uncaptured, into the thirsty ground. Though rain is always celebrated, sometimes it has unfortunate consequences. One day after heavy rain, we ended up water logged and stranded at home because the road was too bad. But that is not the sad part. We had no vehicle because it was being worked on near town. That is not the sad part either. Though we were happy that our cement water cistern tank had just measured 79 inches of water and our 5,000-liter poly tank was full the day before, we were shocked to find only 23 inches left? New leakage? It was enough to bring tears to our eyes.

Living in Jome, we have a bit of a love/hate relationship with rain. It brings so much good and so much inconvenience to our lives. I made a few lists:

On the negative side:
- Instead of rationing water, we ration (solar) power.
- More use of the environmentally unfriendly and expensive diesel-powered generator.
- My glasses fog up due to the pre-rain humidity.
- I perspire profusely.
- Food spoils faster.
- It is buggy.
- Siafu (the biting marching ants) can create havoc if you cross their path.
- More bug-eating Geckos.
- Cat whines more often, asking for help catching gecko.
- Must sleep with mosquito net down.
- Line-dried clothes take longer to dry.
- Must carry rain boots in the car.
- Poor infrastructure results in standing water in cities and towns.
- Standing water breeds malaria-carrying mosquitoes.
- Going to the vegetable market can be a muddy mess, and you may see a scurrying rat.
- Any roof leakage can make a map on a ceiling.
- Some villagers lose their mud homes and must rebuild.
- Travel by road to Dar es Salaam can be precarious
- Goats hate rain, so they look for shelter in our grass huts. Sheep do not care, but we lost all our sheep.

On the positive side:

- I can wash clothes without much rationing.
- I can shower twice a day with rainwater with no trepidation.
- Grazing animals have plenty to eat and drink.
- Chickens are happy chasing bugs all day.
- Farmers are hopeful and begin preparing their farms.
- The landscape is more picturesque, green.
- The tree Saidi calls Christmas tree (because it blooms in December) is full of red flowers.
- It is mango season; plenty of pineapples too.
- Less dust.
- Husband surprises me with pictures of rainbows I missed while sleeping.
- Birds, lots of them, especially the masked weaver bird.
- THERE IS LIFE!

CHAPTER 9

LIVING OFF THE GRID

Water isn't the only thing rationed. We faithfully paid our electricity bill while we rented our house in town, but power was not guaranteed. I was dependent on electricity for cooking, so it did not take long for us to make the decision to buy a powerful generator. The $900 we spent was a great investment. We were blessed to have it. I no longer had to delay meals if there was a power outage.

Whenever we saw that our neighbor's lights are back, we switched back to the grid. For one, it is expensive and impractical to keep an ample supply of gasoline on site. It is also noisy and environmentally unfriendly to rely on gasoline. Still, it was something we needed, so we planned to get hooked up to solar power in Jome when we returned from *hajj*.

Upon our return, Saidi and I visited the only solar shop in Lindi. The owner, Hamisi, had also just made the holy pilgrimage. We thought that was a good sign. Eventually, he sent an electrician to our house in Jome to estimate the cost of installing a solar system big enough for our needs. The electrician reported back to the owner that the job was big.

Hamisi only had a few standard packages, and our estimated need fell beyond the largest one. No one asked specifically what our needs were or about the power requirements of our appliances, especially the biggest monster, the refrigerator. We repeatedly asked for more specifics and follow up. Hamisi had not visited our house personally, and the information from the electrician he contracted was sketchy to say the least. Based on this limited information, he didn't have any good feedback.

After doing some comparative shopping in Mtwara, the relatively more developed city 100 kilometers south of Lindi, we opted for Hamisi's services. We correctly predicted that we would need ongoing maintenance support. The closer, the better. In a country where "buyer beware" holds true and the middleman rarely takes responsibility for defective goods, we thought the shortest distance for transporting fragile panels was best. Plus, Hamisi's top-of-the-line package was comparable to the quote we received in Mtwara.

When Saidi saw Hamisi and another electrician friend at a funeral in Mchinga, he invited them to Jome, which was an 18-kilometer ride on their *pikepike*. This was the beginning of a long trial-and-error, living-off-the-grid process that I suspect may never be fully resolved. It also was the beginning of a meaningful friendship with Hamisi.

Living off the grid in Tanzania is no easy task. It took a lot of work—I mean a whole lot—so I would like to get into some of the details of how we did it. At the start, we identified two phases. First, wire the house. Second, add in the power source, solar with a back-up generator.

We had already promised the first phase to a small independent electrician we used while living in town, but we second-guessed ourselves after meeting Hamisi and envisioning finger pointing when things went wrong. After some thought, we gave both phases to

Hamisi. We said *pole* to the Lindi electrician, and he happily accepted our token payment for his trouble.

In hindsight, this was one of the best decisions we ever made. Nevertheless, there were several other bad decisions that neutralized that good one. To begin, we bought Hamisi's top package: 5 solar panels, a controller, an inverter, change-over switch and 6 batteries. Hamisi trusted us as he allowed us to make payments to finish off our balance. We were constrained by the maximum withdraw limit of the ATM.

When we first moved to Jome, our home was wired for and dependent only on generator power. However, within a week, Hamisi arrived with everything needed to install the solar equipment. I was so excited to see his truck and personal car pull up. Few *fundis* would arrive with their own vehicles. Transport was all part of the deal. For most of the day, Saidi and Hamisi sat in the compound as Hamisi's young *fundis* cut, banged, climbed and carefully navigated the slopes of our roof.

Occasionally, Hamisi would abandon his mostly social conversation with Saidi and call out some instructions in Swahili. I didn't know what he was saying, but I imagined things like, "Wire in parallel to those two batteries." "Wire these two batteries in series." "Connect these batteries to these two panels." "Check the voltage in those batteries."

After it was all done, Hamisi went through the house to read aloud the manufacturer's panels of my appliances. Washing machine? "Yep, it is 350 watts. No problem. You can use solar." Hot water heater? "Better to use generator." Mobiles, computers, TV and satellite receivers? "Solar is fine."

Water pump (to pump to the 2,000 liter tank)? "If it is the only thing you are using, solar is fine." Hamisi continued to follow me around the house as I pointed out our appliances.

Then we went to the kitchen. Cooker? "Oh, this is a lot of watts," he said in his broken English. "Only use the generator." Refrigerator? "No problem, turn on at 10:00 AM and turn off at 3:00 PM."

We were dependent on the generator for pumping water and cooking. From the beginning, though, we had problems, particularly with powering the refrigerator with solar. We could not even support the modest goals Hamisi promised.

All our lighting was AC (alternate current). This meant the inverter converted the DC (direct current) power from the panels and batteries to AC for all of our power needs.

My high school physics came in handy as I recalled that the discovery of AC power changed the world and helped light up cities. Power stations could begin to power cities from remote locations. The electrons, which rapidly alternate direction, power most of the world. My refrigerator, washing machine and most other appliances are powered by AC power. A simple car battery generates DC power, but once you convert DC power to AC power, you've got first-world living. A house powered by a well-designed solar system cannot be distinguished from one on the grid.

Unfortunately, our solar system was not big enough to maintain power through the night. Our battery bank, which stores the power for a rainy day or night, was just too small.

In the middle of the night, Saidi would turn to me and ask, "What time is it?"

"Why?" I asked.

"The lights went out."

I began to call Saidi the light police. He kept track of what time the lights turned off each night and made sure he reported it to Hamisi. Saidi was concerned that this type of setup would cause our external security lighting to cut off in the middle of the night. This prompted Hamisi to rewire the house, putting the lights on DC power, hence bypassing the inverter. We could use all the appliances we wanted without draining the batteries reserved for lights. Problem solved—sort of.

We still had other issues to address. I politely told Hamisi that we did not spend the amount of money we did to merely watch one hour of TV, only to have the power suddenly cut off in the middle of the finale. I was tired of watching only headline news. To remedy this problem, Hamisi suggested we buy three more panels and six more batteries. However, he could only find four more batteries. He also suggested we isolate the refrigerator by putting it on its own mini system with separate inverter batteries and panels.

During one of his visits, we also learned that the original inverter Hamisi sold us did not work on our updated system, so he swapped it out for another. To add to our inverter problems, the small inverter he brought to isolate our refrigerator was not powerful enough, but we had no choice but to exclusively use since he had already removed the main one.

Eventually, he did replace it with a better one. I was happy for the newer inverter because the previous one had a buzzer. Every night, we had to go downstairs, no matter how tired we were, and shut the inverter off manually. I teased Hamisi about this, calling it Hamisi's system. Through my hand motions and broken Swahili, he seemed to understand my point. I could tell he could imagine the nighttime routine Saidi and I had reluctantly adapted to. I sensed a brief moment of compassion.

During this time, we could only cool the refrigerator with the generator. Eventually, after spending thousands of dollars, going through various rounds of trial and error, and a lot of frustration, we ended up with 10 batteries, a different inverter, eight panels and separate AC/DC systems. Things were finally improving, at least temporarily.

It didn't take long for more problems to emerge. Finally, I went to Amazon.com and ordered four books on solar energy, including The Complete Idiot's Guide to Solar Power. If the professionals couldn't fix it, I would figure out how to do it myself. After some reading, I began to question the mish-mash models of batteries and the new-ness of our equipment (specifically the inverter and batteries). In parallel, I began investigating solar refrigerators but opted against it due to cost. I learned from my reading about periodically equalizing batteries by charging them with the generator.

One day, I walked into Hamisi's store with my new books under my arm. I pulled out a table I made that estimates our total energy use. Each appliance, its wattage, and hours used daily were listed. I wondered why we did not do this first. With Saidi standing next to me, I went through my calculations. "350 watts x 2 hours…" I said, letting my voice trail off. Saidi tugged at me, knowing I was backing Hamisi into a corner. "Let's go," he said. "Hamisi is very busy."

Hamisi actually seemed interested in my books, but he couldn't read English. I actually began to admire him for being in a business in which most literature is not in his native language. With Saidi's coaching, I turned it down a notch and began to realize that our power needs were higher than most of Hamisi's customers. I did not want our business relationship to affect our friendship, so we quietly engaged The Pastor, another small solar distributor in the village of Mchinga.

For a couple thousand dollars, The Pastor delivered a brand new, in-the-box-with-manual inverter made in Europe. He installed it, but we could not get the generator to charge the batteries during testing. The Pastor consulted Ahmed, an expert from Dar who arrived a few days later at our expense. (We paid for his transportation and hotel.) He suggested testing the inverter on the grid. The conclusion was that our generator was not powerful enough to make the inverter kick over to charge the batteries.

Ahmed also did an assessment of our batteries. He found that the last batteries Hamisi installed were garbage. Based on the model, Ahmed and The Pastor suspected the batteries were used and some-how made it to the underground market. Ahmed reconfigured our system with the four good batteries and new inverter. He also advised us to buy two new batteries of the same model. Hamisi shied away from this as he knew we were emotionally spent on the battery issue and did not want to jeopardize our relationship anymore by selling us subpar batteries. Ahmed agreed to search for them in Dar.

When it was time for my bi-annual trip to the United States, I planned a surprise visit back home. After I flew to the US, Saidi drove straight through to Jome from Dar the next morning with Ahmed and the window contractor, Omari. Ahmed installed the new batteries and a new controller, and Omari took window measurements. Then, Saidi took them to Lindi to a hotel and gave them bus fare to return to Dar.

It may seem strange to Americans to directly pay a contractor's travel expenses, but it is no different than paying a delivery fee, a service fee, or any other fee that often gets lumped into the price—sometimes without the customer's knowledge.

While in America, I had planned to meet up with an ex-colleague, a renewable energy junkie. I was hoping to gain some valuable info I could take back to Jome. I took the 30-minute drive to his rural home, stopping once for directions. "It is the house with the big wind mill," I was told. Despite the distance, I made it a point to arrive *mzungu* time (i.e., on time).

I knocked several times. No answer. Finally, I called his mobile. "I am so sorry. I forgot," he said. He called his wife by phone, and a few minutes later, a groggy-eyed Caucasian woman in dreadlocks answered the door. Wow, still sleep at 10:00 AM? I hadn't done that in years! She showed me the equipment in their basement that supported their solar and wind-powered systems. She was gracious enough to let me take pictures, but I quickly realized it would be nearly impossible to replicate this system in Jome. I scratched it off my to-do list and resolved myself to working with Hamisi, The Pastor, and Ahmed.

Hamisi seemed happy to see us resolving our energy problem. He looked like he had been losing sleep over it. By the time I returned from the States, he and Saidi had made a deal. Saidi received compensation for the bad batteries, and Hamisi sold our smaller inverter and generator for us. We bought a monster used generator from Hamisi, one that had been used to power a small hotel. By the time all the bartering was over, we paid about two grand for it.

When I say the generator was a monster, I really mean monster. It took six strong men to lift it out of a pick-up truck. There was no need to chain lock it like the other one. Any thief who could move it without being noticed deserved a round of applause. Unlike our previous generator, this one ran on diesel. We fired it up and it charged the batteries. Progress.

Because of our beautiful, but technologically unfriendly, ocean-front environment, other problems arose: wiring with the generator, night time stoppage issues, leaking areas. With every improvement came a new challenge.

The generator battery wouldn't stay charged, so we decided to install a solar panel to help out. My view of solar panels was that they should be on the roof. That's what I had seen in America. Hamisi, too, planned to install them on the roof. However, Saidi was reluctant to agree because our roof was a big investment. The tiles were imported. Additionally, the poles the panels sat on were tall, and we were concerned about the high velocity wind from the ocean.

As it turns out, the holes made for the poles brought leakage. We also had to deal with the banging of a loose panel. Saidi's trepidations were realized. Would our expensive, imported tiles be damaged? Luckily, the loose panel was easily fixed. The leaking roof, which required the replacement of two gypsum ceiling boards, was not as easily fixed.

Hamisi tried twice to stop the roof leakage himself. Even Saidi made the dangerous trip up onto the roof at least once, only to come back down with black caulking goo all over his hands. Eventually, we called our roof guy in Mtwara, who informed us that the distributor of the roof tiles has a foam poly sealant. It would be perfect for our trouble spots, and one of his guys had just come from a seminar on its use. We sent the bus fare and cost of the material by mobile phone. One hour after their arrival, the problem was fixed. Or so we thought. Months later, the leakage started again and we finally all agreed, the poles had to be shortened. Hamisi gladly complied.

As the angle of the sun changed, so did our available power. Living nine degrees below the equator, we did not expect a radical difference in power with the changing seasons. We were wrong. We noticed the three newer panels that were on the ground were not receiving sun until almost midday. The shadow from the upper floor of the house impeded the sun. For people who are stretching their every watt, a few hours of shade can have a big impact.

We called Hamisi and told him our problem. Taking the path of least resistance, he suggested we wait it out until the angle returns to a more favorable position. This option we immediately rejected. Within a few weeks, he moved the panels three meters to their new position, which immediately improved our available power. I guess being the only two-story house in the area comes with its challenges.

As time passed, we learned more and more about how most efficiently and comfortably to live in Jome. One of the biggest quality of life improvements was purchasing a timer for the refrigerator. Prior to the timer, we had to turn the power off whenever we left for town. We had adjusted to six hours of refrigeration. All drinks were stored in the freezer, and fresh vegetables and fruit were stored in the lower refrigerator compartment. It was unpleasant though, arriving home from a long day under the equatorial sun to a refrigerator of hot drinks. The timer changed everything.

All of this work we put into our home has its worth. During Ramadan, we invited several families to stay the night and have *iftar* with us. No one took us up on the offer. I realize now that the transportation cost was probably a problem for most of our invitees—that or they just did not feel comfortable staying at a *mzungu*'s home.

Hamisi was one of the recipients of our invitation, but he decided to come for the festive day of Eid instead. He said he would come with about 10–15 people. I prepared a meal of rice, goat and vegetables. After finishing Eid prayer in the village, I came home to finish preparing.

They arrived in midmorning from Lindi town. To my surprise, more than 20 bodies poured out of five cars, including the *imam* from the Lindi city center mosque and Hamisi's brother visiting from Oman. I had not expected so many people. Would the food be enough? Hamisi quickly put my mind to rest as he showed us a trunk full of food and drinks. We barbequed on the beach, and I supplemented with the food I had prepared. The wives cooked rice as well and prepared salad onsite. Jome came alive. In the evening, the house was lit up from Hamisi's system.

Later, Hamisi would play an important part in the planning and creation of the LIFT foundation, our non-profit. He always says that if it is for God, he cannot say no. Now, given the built-in challenges of living off the grid, I realize it would have been even more difficult without Hamisi and his friendship. Saidi and I are thankful for his presence. When the usual power outages occur in Lindi, I happily tell Hamisi, "We have power in Jome."

I was tickled to observe as he became more and more comfortable communicating with me in his broken English. Hamisi and his wife are among the few people who do not laugh at me when I try to speak Swahili. I truly appreciate that.

CHAPTER 10

WHAT IS A FUNDI?

It was a bitter sweet day. I had packed up my life in Michigan and was ready to start fresh in Tanzania with my new husband. As I sat in my empty home, which still had the For Sale sign in the yard, the finality of it all began to sit in. I was really leaving. My family, my friends, and the house I had grown to call home—I was leaving it all behind.

Up until that point, I had been so busy packing and preparing that I hadn't even been still enough to fully absorb the magnitude of the change. I was leaving everything I had known behind to start a new life in a new country with a new man. It was a weird mix of excitement and sadness. No doubt, I knew seeing Saidi again would fill some of the void, but I also knew I would miss those being left behind. As we say in Swahili, *Karibu* Tanzania.

Once I arrived in Tanzania again, I immediately knew I had made the right choice. Any sense of doubt and anxiety melted away. This chance at a new life was invigorating. I was relieved that I had neatly wrapped up my past and owed no one anything. I had a fresh start on life. My prayers had been answered and I felt blessed.

While the house was being built in Jome, we traveled there every two days or so to make sure the builders had everything they needed and the folks who were clearing the road (in preparation for the water drilling truck and to minimize tire ware) were progressing. We knew living in Jome would mean having to drill for water. It was a huge undertaking, but it was necessary to have the quality of life we wanted.

We negotiated with two different drilling companies. The one we selected reduced its price by more than half. After all, Saidi had taken one of their employees to the hospital when he had malaria. They were obviously thankful. Many of the building materials were from the area, a strategic move that injected resources into the local economy. Everyone wanted some type of job from us, and we helped as much as we could.

The harmony I witnessed among our Jome workers verified the beauty of Tanzanian culture. In fact, the world could take a lesson from our approach. Yes, we had our occasional setbacks, but our team of revolving *fundis* was a representation of the peacefulness of Tanzanian society and the vision of the government to maintain a country free of tribal, religious and sectarian strife. It truly was inspiring to watch.

Our initial builder was Christian, but his helpers were Muslim. Except for The Pastor, our electricians were Muslim. Hamisi introduced us to our second plumber Jackson, a Christian from Lindi. Our roofer was a Seventh Day Adventist and did not work on Saturdays, but his helpers were Christian and Muslim. Our meticulous painters were a Christian-Muslim duo. Our metal *fundi* was a Bible-carrying member of the Sukuma tribe with a thriving business in Lindi. He introduced us to our mason Rashid and Tano the carpenter.

Juma Choo brought his helpers from Mtwara, but we often had to escort them back to the bus station because they were always drunk. Luckily for us all, they eventually sobered up. I suspect Musa, Juma's team member who we eventually decided to stick with, was numbing the pain of his labor by associating closely with Bangi. Each *fundi* contributed to what I call home today.

In Swahili, *fundi* means "craftsman." Our electricians, masons, plumbers, computer repairmen, welders, generator repairmen, satellite dish installers, window installers, carpenters, mobile repairmen and painters are all *fundis*. (Swahili grammar note: Technically, *fundis* is not a word. The correct plural spelling would be *mafundi*, but no need to be technical here.)

Most *fundis* have no formal education training. I knew that up front, but I assumed their on-the-job training would suffice. Boy, was I wrong! To say I was naive would be an understatement. We had to manage every phase of the project. In most cases, we had to buy and arrange for the delivery of all the materials ourselves. I had no idea how hands-on house building a home in rural Tanzania would be. I now know this is the norm.

On a more positive note, finding *fundis* was relatively simple. Because the communities are close knit, *fundis* are often found through recommendations and word-of-mouth advertising. Once the word was out that we needed workers, they were easy to find.

We selected James for the construction of the house. He was recommended by Ibrahim. We met Ibrahim through Abdullah, who was a good friend of Saidi's deceased nephew. When I first met Ibrahim, I read a bit too much into his name. Because the name has versions in all three monotheistic religions, I assumed it was a good sign. Then I learned Ibrahim owned a bar. I tried to reserve judgment, but I was surprised that someone who was an obvious Muslim could openly profit from something *haram*. I put that aside and figured God would judge us all. After all, we had a house to build.

Once James was officially hired, we needed to have a sit-down to discuss what we had in mind. We arranged to meet him at our rental home in Lindi town. We gave him plenty of creative liberty but told him we wanted something similar to our honeymoon bungalow, which had a upper level and a clear view of the ocean. Looking back, so many things could have gone wrong, but James was a competent engineer. He was one of the few who went to a trade school for his profession.

He admitted he had never built a structure with an upper level before, but he had been trained on how to do so. He was confident he could build our home to our specifications. We gave him our trust. He gave us his amazingly affordable price. I thought, am I getting a house built for the cost of one week's pension? As they say, the devil is in the details. We had no written contract; just an African agreement. Overall, we lucked out.

I didn't want to rely on luck again though, so I began to write contracts after our experience with James. After all, I am a certified professional project manager (PMP). Just because I am retired does not mean I have to throw out all those years of training. I did not use Microsoft Project, but I did track all costs in Microsoft Excel and intuitively redirected the project as the critical path changed. We agreed to what supplies we would have to have at the site before James started: water, sand, stones and bricks.

Weeks later, James arrived before the bricks with his helpers from the town of Masasi. It would take time for him to lay the stone foundation. While the team meticulously laid rope out to define the area that would become my home, Saidi and I strategized about how to get bricks to Jome. The load would be heavy, and only the most daring of drivers would venture to Jome with such a heavy load. We needed someone skilled and fearless.

The search for bricks was the easy part; transport was not as easy. Eventually, James said he could make the bricks at a higher quality and lower price. Subsequently, we had two molds made in town and assured he had the necessary cement, sand and water. He assured us he could get the job done, and he did.

I was quickly indoctrinated into the Tanzanian economy: labor is cheap and fuel is expensive. James made steady progress on the house, but it was all consuming. So they wouldn't have to waste time and money traveling home every day, James and his team stayed in the grass *banda* we had built there. They bought fresh fish and had a woman from a nearby village cook for them once a day. James was in charge of all local labor. We were busy enough. We did not want to be involved in hiring people for different jobs, especially since many of the locals are Saidi's relative. We paid James, and James paid the laborers.

From there, we began to hire trucks to bring water to Jome. Saidi has the natural instinct to trust but verify, so we instructed James to measure the water level before he slept and in the morning to make sure it was not being taken. We also hired a truck to bring bags of cement, quarry stones and steel support rods. James said he had everything he needed for a while except wood, which was being worked on by villagers in Mchinga.

Saidi's boyhood friend, Mohamed, helped manage the preparation of coconut wood that was used temporarily during the building process. We hired the Ruvu *imam*'s dhow to bring wood 18 kilometers across the Indian Ocean coastline from Mchinga to Jome. Days later the tide rose, and eventually the water became high enough for the dhow to leave. I am always amazed at how the people here can predict the natural cycle of the ocean.

The only problem was that Saidi and I had to wait for the water to recede. Saidi was adamant about not driving the car through salt water. "Do you want to kill our car?" he'd ask me anytime I suggested we drive through. The road to Jome was a big problem. It flooded a lot. The local parliament member made no real efforts to fix it. He paid the price by not being reelected.

Because many of the *fundis* were poor, we had to find the most efficient way for them to get money back home to their families. What worked best was buying prepaid mobile phone vouchers. The *fundi* could then forward the airtime to their family, who could then sell it. The majority of Tanzanians do not have a bank account or credit card, but the movement of money through various registered mobile services is constantly expanding.

As things moved along, we made it a point to relax when we could. It was a lot of work managing the building process. We needed to take a rest. We had a second *banda* being built on the property, but we decided to also buy a tent. We wanted to be able to get that camping feel, despite the fact that neither of us are campers. It took us every bit of four hours to put it up. What do you expect? I told you we aren't campers.

The next day, we slept in the tent, Saidi's first time in 40 years. It was breezy in the evening and, as James told me, there were no mosquitoes in Jome. I was relieved as my first bout with malaria was catastrophic. All night, we could hear the gentle lull of the ocean and the moon was almost full. The stars shone down on us as we ate a delicious red snapper we had cooked for us by locals. The only seasoning was the salt from the ocean. It was more than enough. We were in the 10th day of fasting for Ramadan, and the fish complemented some of the rations I brought to break our fasts. It was a perfect night. Saidi laughed and pointed out that the night in Jome did not bother me. (Usually, I demanded that we leave the remote area before dark.) Sleeping in Jome was a milestone, a first of many.

We started feeling comfortable leaving Lindi for short getaways. We later learned that the longer getaways were just too tempting even for James's team to resist the urge to steal.

Hajj season was approaching, and Saidi and I had already made our intentions to go. We knew that meant the *fundis* would have a big chunk of unsupervised time, but we had to go. *Hajj* is a requirement on all Muslims who are able, and we didn't want to wait until we were unable. We did our best to prepare our team. We made sure we delivered all the cement and steel necessary to keep the project going while we were away.

Saidi gave instructions to James: "Here is some money to take care of my brother, *Mzee* Ally, in case there is a health emergency," he said, handing over a wad of cash. "Here is money to hire villagers to bring water so construction can continue," he said as he handed over another wad. "We bought your rice, flour and beans, but here is money to buy fish." And with that he handed over the last sum of money. "You are in charge. We trust you. Don't tell anyone we are travelling abroad."

Lastly, Saidi had a question. "Do you intend to leave the site or travel?"

"No, boss, I will be here. We will finish the steps and top floor. Don't worry," James reassured him. But there is a saying here in Tanzania that I absolutely understand now: no hurray in Africa. And as we Americans say, when the cat is away, the mice will play.

Well, not only did they play, but someone helped themselves to some of our building materials (cement, water and steel). Someone also helped themselves to our hand-painted Jome/Ruvu road sign. For some in highly impoverished areas, stealing becomes a means of survival.

When we returned, the progress was not at all what we expected. To be fair, I must point out the things the team did finish in our absence. The steps to the second floor of the house were complete; the walls for the upstairs were done; and the metal security grills for the downstairs windows had been delivered. Despite our disappointment, the show had to go on.

As quickly as we could, we delivered more cement, steel and the rushed order of metal front and back doors. We wanted to make sure we could secure the building materials before James took his Christmas break. We also ordered a grill for the very large upstairs windows. They were relatively pricey but long overdue.

We later found out that James made a trip home to Masasi while we were on *hajj*, leaving his two helpers in charge. That's when our materials began to disappear. One of the helpers conspired with locals to sell our cement—get this— for one-fourth of what we paid! Talk about adding insult to injury.

It took some time to figure out who was responsible. At first, I didn't even think anything was wrong. I assumed the missing materials had been used for building. Saidi was the one who noticed a discrepancy between the amount of materials gone and the amount of work done. Saidi said it would take time, but the truth would eventually come out. It did. James's helpers and all others involved were promptly fired.

We went to Jome Christmas day. Just being there cheered me up. Walking around the peaceful land helped to relieve some of the stress of crunching numbers for the house and digesting the betrayal from James's team, Mr. Stone, Saidi's nephew and Saidi's brother-in-law. Saidi took me to a part of Jome I had never seen. "That is our island over there," he whispered. Technically, it is a peninsula—you can walk there in calf-deep water—but island sounds better. He told me his father was the first human there. He used to fish with nets. The land of Jome is truly special, so I was willing to deal with thieving *fundi*'s to make it our permanent home.

After our experience with Phase 1, we were more hands on. We had to be. One of the first things we did as we began the finishing phase was put up temporary wire fence to secure the compound. We were tired of seeing Jome becoming a hangout for the jobless. Before we discovered who was involved in the cement theft caper, everyone was a potential suspect. We had to toughen up. If you did not have a job in Jome, there was no need for you to be there. It was then that I understood why so many house constructions begin first with the costly brick compound wall.

As the house grew taller and started to look more like an actual house, it became time to construct the roof. I did not picture myself living in a house with the common corrugated metal sheet roof, which would rust in a few years, so we invested in top quality materials from around the world. Our roof tiles were manufactured in New Zealand; they are supposed to be great for our harsh environment. The gutters were manufactured in South Africa. We didn't have to go so far for our roofing materials. While shopping in Mtwara, we were given the number of a roofing *fundi*, Steve. We had planned to go to Dar for the materials, but we were happy to get Steve. This was the beginning of our long relationship with the Mtwara *fundis*.

Steve turned out to be a wonderful choice. He got us a blueprint made of the house, and his team did a great job with the roof. As I strained my neck to watch them work, I got a bit nervous. The young men were as graceful as gymnasts, but they were up so high without any type of tethering. There is no Occupational Safety and Health Administration here.

Steve was happy to oblige when asked if he knew a good plumber, painter and septic digger. After dealing with so many unreliable people from the nearby town of Lindi, we were happy to branch out to Mtwara. Another advantage of bringing *fundis* from Mtwara was that they were virtually trapped in Jome until the job was done. We picked them up at the Lindi bus station, gave them lunch and left them in Jome to work.

Before any *fundi* could get started, we had each of them sign my new contract. Enough of the African way. Saidi explained in Swahili the contents of the contract. I hoped the contracts would cut out all (or at least some) of the chitchat Saidi had to entertain about scope and payments. Before the contracts, we wasted precious time going back and forth with them about requests for advances and other issues. With the contracts, they knew we were serious. Every little payment got subtracted on paper from the amount due. We managed everything: getting materials, tending to each teams' needs and feeding people. It was taxing, but it was for our own good. Someone had to ensure that things got done. Who better than us?

For the most part, we were very happy with Steve. However, like most people here, he delayed giving bad news. When we arrived in Jome, the roof tiles were almost done. We brought our generator so they could use a power saw to cut the corner tiles. Things were progressing smoothly. Saidi and I relaxed in our beach *banda*, listening to the banging and sawing. I couldn't relax for too long, though. "Something is wrong," I said. "The noise has stopped."

Saidi was not worried. "They know what they are doing. They are not children."

"I am telling you, I do not hear the generator or saw," I insisted. I couldn't let it go. After some prodding, Saidi eventually went to the house. Upon his return, he informed me that they underestimated the number of tiles and were short by about 35. Had they told us earlier, we could have called Dar and began arranging payment and transport before supplies ran out. But because they waited until the absolute last minute to tell us, work came to a standstill. After leaving Jome distraught, we received a text from our roof *fundis* asking for money. Talk about bad timing! In one day, we sent emails to Dar for a reorder, made bank deposits, scanned receipts and arranged transport from Dar for the additional roof tiles.

With the help of one of Saidi's brothers, we received the needed materials within a few days. That seems like a reasonable amount of time given the circumstance, but Steve and his crew were ready to leave by then. We arrived just as they were piling into another worker's pick-up to return home. It was Friday night and two of them were 7th Day Adventists, so they did not work on Saturdays. We respect everyone's religious beliefs, but this was a problem they created for themselves.

We were tough and told them we would get someone else if they left. The final compromise was that two would stay and two would return home to observe the Sabbath the next day. To add to the confusion, we were also managing the building of a local house for Saidi's oldest brother, *Mzee* Ally, and his new wife.

Though we had signed contracts with all our new workers, we had not yet signed any with our *choo* guys. We had been consumed with the riskier roofing project. They were hired to replace Mr. Stone, and it never dawned on us to sign contracts with hole diggers. There were no expensive materials to buy, just maintenance of a rudimentary stake and mallet. Even though they were recommended by Steve, we considered the team on probation, waiting to see how they would perform. At the time, we did not realize how important their job would be in determining our move-in day.

Choo is the Swahili word for toilet. It is also the name saved in Saidi's phonebook on his mobile for our head choo *fundi*. Saidi reminded me, "Don't call him Mr. Choo in front of him." Certainly, he would not find it as amusing as we did.

One day, one of Mr. Choo's assistants came back to Jome drunk from another village, the same village that was the recipient of our stolen cement. He was belligerent with the others about some missing chili peppers he had purchased. We have no tolerance for drunkenness, so we told him he'd have to leave the site the next day with Mr. Reliable, our delivery guy. Once we got a contract in place with Mr. Choo, the cost for transport of the drunk was subtracted from his profit and the incident was documented. We had to make it clear that we meant business.

With everything we'd been through, I did not even want to think about Phase 3 until the Phase 2 guys were finished and out of the way. Phasing the project helped keep it under control. It made the process less intimidating, more manageable. The house was finished, almost. Our toilet became the focal point. We moved Mr. Choo from digging the water cistern to the septic. I informed Saidi I would not be going into the woods with a shovel like the *fundis*. There are many modern amenities I can live without. A flushing toilet is not one of them. Nine months after we started construction, the toilet was done. Mr. Choo stayed onsite another two months to dig what would become the water cistern. We would be moving in soon.

As all homeowners know, the story does not end there. It never does. We quickly learned that the open window plan did not work. Begrudgingly, we began to accept that the expensive wood frames were an unneeded expense; the wire in the frames rusted. It was the cost we paid for not being experienced and being too trusting. The design was perfect in good weather, but every time we received a downpour of rain with wind from the east, we had to mop up a small lake inside the house. We thought we could take a break from major construction, but the day I slipped on a wet floor coming down the steps, we agreed to bite the bullet and put in glass windows.

We initially tried working with a Lindi *fundi*, but his delays were frustrating. We opted for someone from Dar. Thanks to Mtwara Corridor and Mr. Reliable, we were able to get the aluminum frames and glass to Jome with little damage.

We continued our relationship with our founding *fundis* for needed repairs and maintenance, especially our mason Rashid, not to be confused with James's Rashidi. Rashid was initially sent by our metal guy to install the upper floor window security grill, but he mentioned that he could also do tiles. Rashid worked like the Energizer Bunny. I was always amazed by how much progress he made. There is nothing like a hardworking *fundi*.

As hard as our *fundis* work, we often have to roll up our sleeves and join in. We bought and transported all the indoor tiles in our car. I did the house measurements and calculations. I was curious about the accuracy of my measurements and estimates. I wondered if I was off. As it turns out, I had been doing well in my estimates, usually overestimating a bit.

Every time we arrived in Jome to check on the progress, the first thing we noticed was the pile of broken tiles Rashid found in the boxes. We transported them ourselves, so we knew it didn't happen on the ride over. Still, they were broken and useless to us. But, as I've learned, nothing goes to waste in Africa, so we loaded them up and sent them to the village mosque in Ruvu. Saidi decided to buy floor tiles for the mosque. A few weeks later, the Ruvu mosque had a nice tiled floor. But even more amazing was that my broken tiles were used to form a mosaic on the mosque's back deck step. I played a mental game of matching broken pieces to the room they matched in my home.

The wall behind the *minbar*, from where the *imam* gives his Friday *khutbah*, housed the overstocked bathroom tiles. Initially, I fought Saidi about putting them in the mosque, because it reminded me of my bathroom. He reminded me that no one from the Ruvu mosque has ever been in my master bath. Good point. I quickly got over it.

Of all our *fundis*—and there were a lot—Rashid is one of our favorites. Some of our fondest memories are from our time with him. He was hardworking and never complained about the austere conditions in Jome. Even with no power, no toilets and no running water, he never complained. He and the other *fundis* gathered their own firewood and did their own cooking. Most slept on straw mats on the dirt ground. Their *banda* was made of grass, and, depending on the phase, it was crowded with several snoring, smelly *fundis*, rats, monitor lizards and the occasional snake. Yet, they seemed to enjoy the peace of the ocean, the access to cheap fresh fish and octopus, and an unlimited amount of flour, beans and rice.

The *fundis* in the later phase had it easy. They got to move from the *banda* into a shell of a brick house. But after the tiles were laid, they all had to vacate and move back into the grass *banda*, at least until we had completed auxiliary local houses in Jome.

Rashid did the finishing of our house, installed all our tiles. Rashid also helped with the toilet after Mr. Choo finished. He built the septic and cement cistern from the big holes Mr. Choo dug. Three years after meeting Rashid, he built one of our biggest quality of life improvements: the brick compound wall.

It is amazing how things changed after our brick wall and metal gates were put in place. The number of people coming to house watch dropped, or so it seems. Those who still come can sometimes catch a peek into the top rooms of the house from afar, but that's about it. The house feels so much more spacious and fitting for a modest woman like myself. I can now venture outside the walls of my house into my compound without putting on my *hijab*. That's a big deal. Any time a Muslim woman finds a private space where she is free to uncover, it is a big deal.

In the end, it took more money and time than we estimated, but we did it. We moved to a remote, abandoned area in rural Tanzania and built a two-story home with plumbing and off-grid electricity. Even with all the delays, setbacks, wasted money and thieving *fundis*, it was worth it to create something of our own in a place as special as Jome, Saidi's homeland.

As we became more and more comfortable in Jome, our little getaways became less frequent. It seemed no one had anything better to offer than what we already had.

CHAPTER 11

THE LAND

I do not know why, but it seems indigenous peoples are late in understanding that land has a tradable value. Maybe it is because there is so much of it. Southern Tanzania has vast unoccupied land that is under the control of villages. The people see the unoccupied land as something they all own, something they all have a stake in. And that's a beautiful belief to have, but it created a vulnerability when people from a more individualistic culture, like European colonists, come along with their rigid ownership rules and ulterior motives. This is exactly what happened to Tanzania, the rest of Africa and many other places across the globe.

European colonist took advantage of peoples that looked at land collectively, as a gift from the Creator to be shared and respected. By the time the Africans and Original Americans woke up, it was too late. Their land and power was gone. Colonists have since left, but their legacy lingers. In the Motherland, Europeans were often replaced by revered strongmen with socialist ideologies. Eventually, the pure socialist model collapsed to be replaced with a capitalist one. Nowadays, these ex-colonies, for the most part, do not have the systems or good governance in place to manage their most precious resource, the land.

Villages that are rich in land, and potentially minerals, are at the mercy of a cumbersome, paper-based bureaucratic system to protect them from land speculators from abroad and within. Some investors are well-meaning. Many African countries welcome outside investors and see it as a path to prosperity. However, some leaders conspire with greedy investors to get what they can before their tenure is up. Those countries that rejected all foreign investors as a reaction to a very exploited past have suffered the consequences. They were left with a void: no equipment, no factories, no skilled labor and extreme poverty.

Seventy-five percent of Tanzanians live in rural villages. Most rural village dwellers do not have the education, capital or management skills to develop their land. Few have electrical power or running water, and many villages are still only accessible by bicycle. This simplistic way of life is not necessarily bad, but it creates sanitation problems and makes it harder for industries to develop. Things are slowly changing, but this substantial segment of Tanzanian society remains vulnerable and at the mercy of the economically and politically powerful.

Land disputes involving this vulnerable population appear daily in the local news. Some of the biggest land disputes are between the pasturalists and farmers. Pasturalist communities depend on their large herds of cows, goats and sheep for their livelihood. Most famous of them is the raw-meat-eating, blood-drinking Maasai tribe. You've probably seen pictures or a National Geographic segment on them. They are known for their tall height, colorful beaded jewelry, large ear piercing and bright red draped clothing.

When tourists visit the Serengeti, home of the famous children's movie Lion King, they often visit Maasai communities to get a tourist's taste of how the Maasai have lived for centuries.

Like many who depend on the ability to roam free in vast lands, their lifestyle is threatened. The government tries to balance environmental and preservation concerns, the need for development, the tourist dollars and the harmony between competing tribal interests. Like most vulnerable and powerless people, the Maasai often lose.

The pasturalist tribes are indigenous to the northern regions of Tanzania, which borders Kenya. A similar tribe, the Sukuma, is the largest tribe in Tanzania. However, when a group of Sukuma, according to the government, threatened the environment with their large herds, they were told to move. They were given several choices and chose an area in Lindi district about 90 kilometers from Jome. They selected the area primarily because of its open grazing land and, more important, its proximity to a river. Before their arrival, it was rare to see villagers indigenous to the southeast coast with cows. That has changed. We even bought our first Jome cows from the Sukuma.

We continue our relationship with our Sukuma neighbors, especially during Eid-ul-Adha. They are usually the only people who have a large enough herd of goats and sheep to meet my Eid orders. Thanks to my Muslim sisters and brothers in the US looking to make their obligatory donations, the LIFT foundation is able to distribute meat to many of the villagers in rural Tanzania each year. We live peacefully with our Maasai and Sukuma neighbors. I hope the changing landscape doesn't threaten their livelihood any more than it already has.

Rural dwellers are not the only ones at risk when it comes to land ownership. People all over Tanzania get into disputes over who owns what. The news is full of stories about feuding "owners" who claim the same land. Even though most Tanzanians believe they own a piece of the vast country, few have deeds to prove it, and little land has been surveyed.

Most land is acquired by petitioning the village committee. Many claims are based on an ancestral presence on the land (e.g., "My grandpa used to live here," or "My grandmother farmed here"). The government usually respects these claims, after a small process and the payment of fees of course. Typically, members of the village land committee are paid a small fee to attend a meeting regarding the piece of land at hand. The handwritten meeting minutes are then given to the claimant and land ownership is usually granted. Sometimes an entire village meets.

This is how Saidi started the process for Jome. Jome had been unoccupied since 1968, when Saidi's father died and his mother and younger siblings vacated. There was no dispute. "The owner has returned," the villagers exclaimed upon our return. The village meeting minutes stated, "A goat after breaking his rope will eventually return home; and Saidi, like a goat, has returned home with his wife."

Most Tanzanians lived like Saidi's family before Tanzanian's 1961 independence, that is, with extended family on pristine farmland near water. However, in an effort to bring roads, education and healthcare to a spread out population, President Julius K. Nyerere instituted a program called *Vijiji Vya Ujamaa* (Village Family), his form of agrarian socialism. People were herded into designated areas under the watchful eye of armed police, forming the villages that stand today. Some people, like Saidi's father, refused to move. Hence, the small family lived alone in Jome, three kilometers south of the village of Ruvu. That is another reason I felt it was important to live in Jome. It isn't just the land of Saidi's birth. It is Saidi's ancestral land and the final resting place for many that came before.

Nyerere's plan seemed logical. The problem is, the government has still been unable (or perhaps unwilling) to deliver good roads, quality education and adequate healthcare for a vast majority of its citizens.

Fortunately, some residents have realized the importance of having their ownership claims officially documented. Those with the means and the will try to navigate the system to obtain government land deeds, but it isn't easy. Starting with the village meeting minutes, they get the land surveyed. Then they wait. If they are lucky enough to get through that process, they wait for a series of meetings between government employees to approve the petition at the district, regional and national levels. A big milestone is when the land officer schedules the site visit for a nine-member, government-appointed district land committee. Of course, this visit does not occur until some mysterious fees are paid. The petitioner is at the mercy of the land officer—a poorly paid, over worked, powerful government employee.

Knowing it would be a drawn-out task, Saidi started this tedious process when we first made the decision to move to Jome. Amazingly, the survey stones were laid within a week. The survey map, however, took a year. The official report: Jome consisted of 92 acres of farmland and forest. In between, Saidi visited the land office at least monthly to get updates and in return was given assurance that the process was going well.

The visit by the nine committee members came two years later. In between, we were told to get new meeting minutes from both Ruvu and Mchinga. Why these new minutes were needed, I do not know, but Saidi obliged the land officer every step of the way, paying the requested fees without hesitation. He was willing to do whatever it took to secure Jome as our own private space.

To this day, the national land deed has still eluded us, but we have been told "it is going well." I resolved myself to the fact that, when I am dead and buried, none of this will matter.

Despite the lengthy waiting times, there is very little paperwork required when land transfers hands in rural Tanzania. There are no title searchers, insurance agents or realtors. In fact, there is an element of squatters' rights, which is why disputes are so frequent.

Even here in Jome, we had a series of opportunists make claims on our land. At the start of the Jome process, a man identified himself as a grandson of someone who used to live in Jome. His grandfather had been invited by Saidi's father to live there. Seeking the quickest resolution, Saidi agreed to pay a set amount for the family to relinquish their claim. Of course, there had been no interest in Jome until Saidi arrived with his *mzungu* wife, but that is to be expected.

About a year later, we had another group of visitors, some who made the 460-kilometer trek all the way from Dar. The group claimed that the person who took compensation for the land was from the maternal side; they were from the paternal side. Outraged but still measured, Saidi called the village secretary. The land their grandfather lived on is now sand and rock. There is no farm or anything of obvious value. Nevertheless, we agreed to pay some money for their claim. They assured us the problem was permanently resolved.

One year later though, the Ruvu village chairman said he had a letter from yet another descendant of the Jome squatter. Another one? "Just how big is this man's family?" I thought. Fortunately, the chairman sent him away with the instruction to either see his family members who had already received compensation or go to court. The family knew going to court could result in jail time for extortion. We, on the other hand, had all our official, handwritten, signed agreements. We were ready. The parade would have been never ending if we did not stop it. Years later, I am proud to report that I have yet to hear about any other descendants of the Jome squatter.

Sometime later, we found out the government was planning a new city just north of Lindi town. The unsurveyed land used to be a sisal farm during Lindi's better days. After the demise of the sisal farm, the government gave residents the right to farm the land as long as they didn't plant anything permanent. Most people farmed millet, corn and sesame. Others planted cashew trees.

Mr. Gazelle's deceased father had an area in this location. Finally, when the government wanted to use the space for building, it offered to pay residents to relinquish their land. Mr. Gazelle made a series of visits to get his name on the list. Payouts were made at the Tanzanian Postal Bank. In the end, his family was compensated 10,200,000 TZS (about $6,375) for 14 acres. This was divided among 10 children and

3 wives. Mr. Gazelle's share was about $400. The reality of government payouts is rarely as lucrative as it initially appears.

When it comes to offering payouts to residents, the government usually values the land based on its number of cashew trees or coconut trees. Most Tanzanians realize this, so they hurriedly plant a cash crop when they buy land.

Soon after Mr. Gazelle's $400 payment, we heard about an uncharacteristic, well-defined land offering by Lindi City Council. They were selling plots in the new city of Mitwero. The offering seemed like a transparent process: ads were placed on TV, glossy colorful flyers were printed with pictures of the ocean view and prices were established upfront. Wanting not to be left out, Saidi applied for an area. Would this be our home away from home?

As advertised, we received notification via text message that our application was accepted and that we could pick up our official notification at the government-owned bank. The notification stated the cost and square meters of the plot. We had 30 days to deposit the funds. Like many other applicants, we paid sight unseen and waited for roads, power, water and sewage. To this day, nothing has developed. It is still vast open ocean-side land. The government compensated farmers, including Mr. Gazelle's family, for the land, but now there is concern that they were undercompensated.

Since we moved to Jome, the southeast coast regions have become a flurry of activity and speculation. Now when locals see a *mzungu* in Lindi town, they can no longer assume it is a volunteer aid worker. There is an increased presence of Chinese workers who are working on road, construction, and agriculture projects. *Mzungu*s from all around come looking for the perfect piece of coast to invest in and become richer off of. If they're rich enough, investors offer cash payments and promises of new homes, schools, health clinics and mosques—anything to get their hands on this precious African soil, which, ironically, has brought little financial stability to its indigenous inhabitants. Funny how that works.

The village of Kijiweni is located 10 kilometers north of Jome. It has the most beautiful beaches I have seen in southern Tanzania. Kijiweni does not appear to be affected by the dramatic changes of the tide. Unlike Ruvu or Jome, it appears to always be at full tide, an invitation to beach lovers to folly in its blue water and white sand. Its shores are clear, not cluttered by bottles or other washed up debris that beaches usually have. Kijiweni is often called *Jiwe la Mzungu*, the stone of the *mzungu*, so called because of the stone placed there by the Portuguese to mark the northern border of what is today the country of Mozambique.

The stone is no longer there. It was removed by Germans who wanted to claim the land for themselves. After all, colonists from all over Europe fought for centuries for slices of Africa to add to their empires.

A century later, Kijiweni is still an area of substantiated anticipation. Villagers go about their daily life. Thatch-roofed mud houses align the main road as they have for decades. There is one exception to this commonality, the occasional visit by *mzungu*s to their relatively permanent campsite at the far end of the beach.

Everyone wonders what will become of this beautiful place. A rich American inquired about buying it. Upon hearing the news of a possible buyer, people rushed to build the most modest of mud structures in anticipation of the cash payments promised for each home. I hoped that the investor would keep it natural if the land was actually sold. A "Club Med" atmosphere would be a disaster for the indigenous people. Most likely though, it would be for visitors looking to commune with nature at a hefty price. That would be OK by me.

Later, I learned that the American wanted to set up a reserve, lions and all. Saidi and I often discussed the possibility of a restaurant nearby. It would be somewhere else to go when we wanted to venture off our homestead. Villagers agreed on the offers presented to them; but the economic climate led to the deal falling apart, at least for now.

To this day, rumors are still circulating about what will happen. We shall see what becomes of it all.

It was no rumor that there was interest in my own village of Ruvu. A rich Arab Tanzanian paid 1,000,000 TZS (or about $625) to every household in Ruvu except ours. Even the occupants of our three Jome local houses, located 500 meters north of us, received payment. The villagers signed contracts, most with just a fingerprint, and had their pictures taken. For their homes, they bought corrugated metal sheet roofs, which they soon sold when their stomachs were empty.

Our relationship with our dear village of Ruvu began to deteriorate after this incident. Tempted by the quick cash, they refused to heed Saidi's advice to get a lawyer for the village. Upset with our recommendation, those managing the distribution of the money scratched us off the list. Perhaps they assumed we had no business advising them on what to do since we lived in Jome in our *mzungu* house, or maybe they simply didn't like the idea of anyone telling them to do something that wouldn't immediately put money in their empty pockets. I understand our situations are different, so I try not to judge. I only hope their decisions benefit them in the long run.

Mobiles given by the Arab, as people call him, for use by the village committee were instead sold for quick cash to the benefit of a few. Statements such as "Ruvu sold their village," and "In a few years, Ruvu will be no more" can be heard by outside observers. We heard the Arab asked about the area north of Ruvu, Jome. The land officer responded, "It's taken."

In addition to foreign investors, the military has also had an interest in Ruvu. One day, two cars unexpectedly showed up at our gate. The entourage included our land officer, a colonel and the Lindi district commissioner. I was happy to see that they were not interested in seeing us. They parked at our gate and walked north. Upon their return, and breathless from their walk, I invited them inside our compound for water and juice. I am always excited to have guests that I can converse with in my native language. Yet, I was not shy about trying out a little broken Swahili mixed in with English.

One of our guests asked, "How do you like life here?"

I felt confident enough to make a joke. "Mimi mama nyumbani," I said, meaning "I am a house wife." I continued, "But for most women here, it is hard work. I see women carrying firewood, a baby on her back, and water while her husband walks next to her carrying only a machete."

They all laughed. "True, that is Africa," one said.

They did not linger, because they still had to drive to Kijiweni. We later learned that they were interested in establishing a military base in the coastal area around Ruvu, including Ruvu itself. Ruvu used to be a port for the export of sisal, so this wouldn't be the first time there was a government presence. With regional concerns of piracy, we concluded their interest was to protect the coast from Somali pirates. Little did we know at the time that we sat on a possible natural gas corridor. If true, it would be an important area to protect.

In 2012, large reserves of offshore natural gas were found in the southern regions of Lindi and Mtwara. Trucks can now be seen carrying large pipes between Mtwara and Dar. Our picturesque view dotted with local dhows and fishermen is sometimes disrupted by the presence of gas exploration ships. One thing is for sure: if we are still breathing in the years to come, our surroundings will be different than they were when we first set foot on this isolated land Saidi's family calls home. We just pray it is for the better.

CHAPTER 12

THE GOOD, THE BAD AND THE UGLY

Everything that has happened during my time in Tanzania can be categorized as good, bad or ugly. Thankfully I've had a lot of good, so the bad and ugly are tolerable. In fact, if I had not experienced an overwhelming amount of good when I temporarily moved here for my fellowship, I probably never would have relocated permanently. I thank Allah (*swt*) daily for the good.

Saidi Truck, so named because he owns a truck, is part of what I am thankful for. He definitely falls in the "good" category. He delivered our first-floor window grills while we were on *hajj*. He was also the one who told us James left the building site while we were gone. That tidbit of information helped us discover the thieving culprits. The quality of workers in rural Tanzania varies greatly, but everyone Saidi Truck has recommended has been golden. He's so reliable that we've taken to calling him Mr. Reliable.

What I appreciate most is that he is always there when we need him. With short notice, he delivered whatever we needed to Jome from Lindi. He selected our replacement rooster, and Mr. Gazelle confirmed that the rooster was doing great. He recommended the metal security grill guy, Mr. Metal, who has also proven to be reliable. Mr. Metal even accepted our personal check, something rarely done by Lindi businessmen. He also referred us to a new water truck delivery guy who made same-day deliveries. That is almost unheard of! Four years later, the water truck remains one of the only trucks that will not hesitate to come to Jome.

Saidi Truck, aka Mr. Reliable, was the one who came and rescued us when our car broke down in the bush. On our way back from Jome after a routine visit to check on construction progress, our car stalled. No power and we had left the jump starter charging in the house. Though it was night, there was a full moon, so we had enough light to feel moderately safe. Saidi suggested walking back to Jome and sleeping there, but I was not keen on that idea. I had no interest in making that four-kilometer walk in the dead of night, especially when we had access to a car that was not stuck on a hill or any other unsafe place. Luckily, Saidi got through to Saidi Truck with only one signal bar on his mobile. Reliable as ever, Saidi Truck arrived about 90 minutes later. He brought us two bottles of Coke Cola and a bag of cashews. We exchanged batteries and agreed to meet up the next day to return his battery.

I also found good at the Aga Khan Hospital in Dar. It appears to be the best health facility I have visited in Tanzania. The doctor took time with me and ran lab tests. (I was not feeling well when we went to Dar to buy the roof tiles.) By the time I was done, my bill was a total of about $43, a price too high for most Tanzanians. The doctor had worked in many places (the UK, Poland and Sudan) and was happy to be back in sunny Tanzania. He said he was depressed in the UK because he went to work in the dark and returned home in the dark. Like many other Tanzanians, he thrived on the warmth of the East African sun.

Saidi's niece's husband, Bima, brought more good into our lives. He was the reason our cement stopped walking away. Once the materials started disappearing, he agreed to stay at the building site in Jome, at the Ruvu *imam*'s recommendation. That simple move solved the problem. No more cement walked away. Afterward, we hired him as a Jome guard. He also cooked for the workers and did odd jobs around the site. He stayed with us for a year.

Of course, good would not be recognizable without the presence of bad. Balance in all things, right? Well, the people who ripped us off represent the bad. After we paid our hard-earned money and took our precious time transporting the cement, we couldn't believe that some of our workers (a few of whom were Saidi's relatives) stole it. Perhaps we were naïve to think they wouldn't steal, but we assumed James would be there to supervise the entire time.

Something else that falls into the "bad" category is superstition. Before we found out who had stolen the cement, the word was out that we were determined to find the responsible parties. People were nervous because, regardless of the religion's prohibition of superstitions, many still believe in them. If one goes to the nearby village of Mchinga and pays a particular lady, for instance, people get nervous. Why? Well, let's just say she killed her brother with a curse. That's what people think anyway.

She had given him 50,000 TZS (about $30) of charity money to take to the mosque. Greedily, he only gave 2,000 TZS and kept the rest for himself. After she found out, he got sick and mysteriously died. Everyone assumed she had dabbled in witchcraft. From that point on, people thought they could pay her to make sure others got their just desserts. The thought of Saidi giving that woman money led to their permanent disappearance from Jome, apparently overcome with fear and guilt. Of course, we did not entertain any superstition talk. We just cleaned house and proceeded on.

When I think of the ugly, rats are the first thing that comes to mind. Maybe it is the *mzungu* in me, but a rat or cockroach in the house sets me off more than a snake. I think it is because seeing one is a signal that there are many more.

I will never forget when Saidi caught one in the house we rented in Lindi town. It was the third one in 10 months. Thankfully, Saidi always sees them first even though I usually hear them first. The last rat we encountered in town was in Saidi's clothes closet. He called me from the kitchen as he held the door closed. "Can you come here and bring me a stick?" He paused for a second, unsure of whether or not he wanted to continue. "There is a rat in the closet," he finally said.

"Is it big?" I asked. Like that even matters. I despise all rats.

He didn't answer the question. "Just get me a stick," he insisted. I gave him the stick and made myself scarce. Soon after, I heard banging. When the noise stopped, I wondered if it was running free or if Saidi had conquered it as usual. He showed me the dead rat in a dust pan and I found the pool of blood in the hall. Gross, but at least he was gone. I felt relieved to see evidence of the rat's demise. I then noticed that the rat poison we put out was gone, too. This was comforting. It had been in the same place for months, so I assume the rat was a recent visitor.

Another time, we put poison pellets down and waited for them to disappear. I checked the spot regularly to see if any had been eaten. Finally one morning, some of the pellets were missing. Saidi convinced me that the rat had gone outside to die. We put out more poison for the next intruder, and I tried to put the presumably dead rat out to my mind. It was hard though. He had urinated in my drawer two days earlier.

At about 3:30 AM, I heard something by my closet. The straw mats we used for floor coverings made it easy to hear anyone or anything walking across (even rats).

I nudged Saidi to see if he heard it, too. He did. Aware of my intense and irrational fear of rats, he got up quickly. I knew I would see it this time. Armed initially with the arrow from his bow, he banged around and told me the pellets were gone.

Sure enough, the rat came running out. Our bedroom door was locked, so there was nowhere for the rat to go. My vision was blurred without my glasses, and I was still under the mosquito net. Still, I was amused by the sight of Saidi chasing a rat in his birthday suit. I felt somewhat safe—that is, until I saw it successfully run up the window curtain! I wondered if it could run up the mosquito net, too.

The rat jumped. Saidi grabbed the broom stick and banged it around, hitting the rat. That's when he realized he was winning the battle. With the rat temporarily out of my sight, Saidi yelled, "Got you!" Indeed, he did. My hero. He isn't always my hero though. I remember he told me after a trip once, "Oh, I forgot to tell you there is a rat in the car." Can you believe him? But as they say, no harm, no foul.

If the rats weren't invading our house, they were making themselves at home on our *bandas*. One day, the Jome *fundis* told us they had some unwanted visitors. We picked up some rat poison in Lindi and headed home. By the time we arrived, Bima had already taken matters into his own hands. He pointed out a huge rat he had killed and laid on the beach. "This is a bush rat," Saidi exclaimed.

I couldn't believe my eyes. It was as big as a cat! I asked that the rat be removed from the beach because I did not want to think about swimming with a dead rat that could wash up in the tide. Rashidi buried it. Saidi and I took a long walk and then slept in our *banda*. I felt safe there with Saidi, no longer worrying about the ugly.

A few days after our last rat encounter in Lindi town, I received an article in my inbox from one of my alma maters, Western Michigan University, called "Rat Heroes." A WMU professor found that rats can detect land mines and the TB bacteria. I emailed the professor, and he invited me to see his lab in Morogoro, Tanzania. I guess beauty truly is in the eye of the beholder.

Since we moved to Jome, there has never been a rat in our house. The house is pretty solid thanks to James and his workers. Having a cat may help, too. We know we are surrounded by bush rats, but they never seem to make it inside. I am definitely not complaining.

The verdict was out for a long time on the water drilling company. Were they good, bad or ugly? This situation was complicated, so it was hard to say. Actually, I know for certain they aren't part of the good. That's an easy call, but the rest is a little murky.

Because things were not working out with the water drilling company, we requested a refund. They agreed to pay, but it took them two years. We had a contract for them to drill at the first choice location as determined by the survey. They said they drilled about 20 meters and found fresh water, then found salt water around 30 meters. We decided to drill at another spot and not go so deep once we found fresh water. It was obvious they did not want to do that.

Instantly, the supervisor's attitude seemed to change. He reluctantly moved the equipment to the new site, not too far away, that was selected by the government surveyor. We heard the team drill for only a few minutes before they said they found salt. Then, they packed up, moved out and stopped answering our calls. There was unsubstantiated suspicion that politicians paid them off. After all, how can two individuals get water so easily when the government has done nothing to make it more accessible for the surrounding villages? Elections were just a month away. They couldn't risk being shown up.

Before we left on *hajj*, the drill company finally sent the pump team to take a sample at the original drill site. Our plan was to desalinate, but they said they couldn't get a sample due to its shallow depth of 11.5 meters. We put it out of our minds while on *hajj*, but we went immediately to their office in Dar the day after we came back. Maybe the team did not really drill 30 meters, or maybe someone put rocks in the bore hole to sabotage it. Regardless, we settled on a sea water desalination plan. Why desalinate from a bore hole when the sea is also salty, has unlimited water and is closer to the house? After receiving the lab water test report, we heard nothing.

Frustrated but still interested, we decided to have them come back and drill the 75 meters contracted. To our surprise, they did not mention the sea water desalination plan. They offered to either give us a refund or send a machine after drilling eight bore holes ahead of us. We opted for the refund, which they took two years to issue.

The Lindi land officers are also bad. Just like the water drilling company, they were quick to take money and slow to produce results. In fact, the Lindi water surveyor was likely the ring master behind our drilling failures. Our paths occasionally cross in town, but he knows we will never use him again. Looking back, I feel for the water drilling company. They may have been caught in a no-win situation, so they took the unusual step of refunding all the money we paid. Despite the long wait, they did make good on their promise, so I will categorize them as bad, not ugly.

CHAPTER 13

THE HELP

The cement caper made us realize what we both already knew intuitively: It would be difficult to stay alone in Jome. Even with Saidi's excellent navigation skills that had not weakened in the 40 years he had been gone, we both knew it would not be prudent to stay totally alone. We needed someone (or perhaps a few someones) to help us keep Jome safe.

I met Bima, our first guard, briefly on my first visit to Ruvu. Bima's wife, Moza Hassan, is the daughter of Saidi's half-sister from the slave side (more on that later). When Jome was still inaccessible by car, Moza was one of two people who escorted us there by foot. On our second visit, Bima was our sole escort. He had a local dhow waiting for us to cross the waist-deep salt water. From there, we walked another three kilometers south over rocks and sand to finally reach the Jome mangrove forest. Bima is originally from Mambulu, 30 kilometers away. It was fishing that brought him to Ruvu. He married Moza and blended right in.

Aside from his good heart, something else that stood out about Bima was the fact that he can read and write. This rare skill made him a valuable resource for the village. He could do something nearly no one else in the village could. When the Aga Khan Foundation rolled out its Village Saving and Loan program in Ruvu, Bima was elected the chairperson of one of Ruvu's six groups. After the other workers were long gone, Bima continued to live in the worker's grass *banda*. He was the first person we put on a fixed monthly salary, which helped him make rapid improvements to his house in the village.

He replaced his grass roof with corrugated metal, replaced the dirt floor with cement, added window frames and doors and bought a sofa. I was concerned that, despite his relative improvement in quality of life, he could not enjoy it. He was absent from home day and night, chained to Jome. During farming season, he hired others to dig on his farm. I wondered, with the frequent visitors we received from Ruvu, why didn't Moza ever visit her husband?

One day, Bima informed us that his eight-year-old son's *jando* was approaching. His son, Hamza, did not have any other boys to share in this rite of passage, so we invited him to stay with his father in Jome. The day after his circumcision, Bima brought a sore Hamza to Jome.

For one month, Hamza stayed in Jome. I made a big cup of warm milk for him each day but tried my best to stay away from him. According to their custom, there should not be any contact with women during the healing time. Hamza's experience was not exactly like those of the past, but it was close. Occasionally, elders came to visit, giving passed-down lectures that have remained unchanged for centuries. The local doctor came twice to check on him, but Bima himself took Hamza to the ocean to remove the bandages.

Waziri, the son of the daughter of the son of Saidi's paternal uncle, also joined Bima in Jome. He helped out on odd jobs. Waziri calls me Bibi or Grandmother. We hired Waziri to build several beach *bandas*. However, something was off. With each of Waziri's visits, Bima's enthusiasm seemed to fade. It was strange, but I didn't put too much thought into it. I was fond of them both. They both attended the mosque, and Bima came with us to our first Eid prayer since moving to Jome.

Slowly, I learned that people were teasing Bima. They made jokes about his job duties, especially the animal caretaking. It was obviously jealousy, but it still bothered him. He finally mentioned that he wanted to leave the job to spend more time with his family. We told him that would be fine but to try to give us proper notice.

After Bima, we hired Mr. Gazelle (aka Bangi), our closest neighbor. He was a fixture in Jome from the early days. He did odd jobs for us, the biggest of which was fetching water. He also put the posts up for our wire fence and put fishnet fences around our young coconut trees. Mr. Gazelle had been around from the beginning as he was also the road clearing guy. He initially seemed like a devoted family man, but I began to question that when I noticed his long absences to go farm in another village. Did he not think his family here wanted to see him at least occasionally? Despite the absences, he was a hard worker when he was around. The other villagers complained that he got all the Jome jobs.

Even with Bima and Mr. Gazelle around, we still needed more help because of our plans to buy cows, sheep and goats. We decided to offer Musa, Mr. Choo's helper, a job before he left Jome. He had replaced Mr. Choo's original helpers, who were fired one by one due to their frequent visits to the bar in Kiloambwani.

Under Mr. Choo's supervision, Musa worked hard. Our initial plan was for him to take care of the goats and sheep as well as prepare food for the dogs. We didn't have any goats or sheep onsite when Musa started his new job, and Bima was still taking care of our dog. There wasn't much for him to do, so we kept Musa busy with odd jobs until we could slide him into a more permanent role. When *Mzee* Ally needed water, Musa did it. If we needed to clean the road, Musa did it. He filled in the cracks by doing what Bima and Mr. Gazelle didn't have time for.

Sijoli had also moved to Jome. As much frustration as he brought us, he is family, so we gave him more chances than usual. We were having another house built in case Saidi's mother ever wanted to return to Jome. We allowed Sijoli to be the house warmer; we needed someone to keep it clean and free of snakes. He didn't have a permanent job, so he picked up odd jobs here and there. We didn't mind putting Musa on a fixed salary, but Sijoli was a special case. He wasn't nearly as reliable, so we had to pay him per job. That was the only way to get any work out of him.

Though Musa had proven himself to be a hard worker, we soon learned that his work ethic suffered without Mr. Choo there to supervise. We were surprised to see that he was so unreliable and would often return to his house during work hours. It seemed Sijoli was wearing off on him. The two were often seen in Musa's house together.

Borrowing from my career training, I tried instituting daily update meetings in the evening to review what had transpired during the day and what the upcoming duties were. I gave each person a chance to talk and had Saidi translate. Bima and Musa became more vocal after a few meetings, but Sijoli never seemed to care. Eventually, the meetings ended when no one would arrive on time. That was one of many failed experiments that seemed only to work in corporate America.

I knew that a motivated worker is a good worker, so I tried to find what motivated each member of our team, but it was hard. One day, I asked Mzee Ally if Musa and Sijoli were doing *bangi*. "Sana" (plenty), he told me. That explained a lot. Eventually, Musa and Sijoli became too high maintenance, so we sent them on their way.

Finally, the goats came. Because Musa had already been fired, Bima helped us find a young man named Rashid to care for them. Rashid had some friends who also wanted to come work. We told them we were fine with that as long as they knew they would be sharing one salary. They agreed, so we invited all of them to see where they would be living and working before they made the decision. We wanted them to know what they were getting into. They agreed to the job, and we gave them transport money to return a few days later. They took the money and never returned to Jome.

The job ended up falling into Bima's hands. He cared for the goats and, later, the sheep. Bima also had to carry water for Mzee Ally. Later, Mr. Gazelle told us he had heard Bima was going to leave Jome. He was right. The last time I saw Bima in Jome was the day we gave him his last pay. On that day, he told us he would not be working in Jome any longer. We had no notice.

About a week after Bima left, Saidi asked Moza if she would visit. He wanted to thank her for Bima's service and their family's sacrifice. Moza said she did not know why her husband left; he was quiet when she asked. Others came within weeks, trying to pull out whatever gossip they could, but Saidi was certain not to feed into it. He made sure everyone knew we appreciated Bima's service. He moved to Jome when we were new to the area. He helped us get grounded. The only information Saidi was willing to share with those who inquired was that Bima had been with us a year and that his contract was over. We never got a straight answer on why he left, but he had a new baby son within a year.

Without Musa or Bima, Saidi had no choice but to take care of the goats and sheep himself, at least until we found a replacement. As temporary relief, Mr. Gazelle took Bima's place, and we looked for someone to take care of the cows.

Saidi owned a cow in Ruvu who had recently given birth. He talked repeatedly about bringing them to Jome. With the compound now ready for cows, Saidi was ready to move. We talked to Osama, our Sukuma contact, and agreed to buy two additional cows sight unseen, one of which was pregnant. We knew we needed another caretaker before we brought our new investments home.

On our search to find someone for our cows, we traveled to the nearby village of Mvuleni. Saidi had a relative who had a son who used to take care of cows. However, he declined our offer, stating that he was farming and could not stay in the bush. We later saw the young man fishing, not farming, but did not waste time speculating. If he did not want to do the job, that was all we needed to know.

Eventually, Mr. Gazelle made an offer that would change his life forever. He said he knew someone in Kitomanga who could care for the cows. He left for Kitomanga and called us when everything was final. It seemed like a sound deal, and the guy had already been to Jome. Shortly after, we went to Kitomanga to pick up Mr. Gazelle and his brother-in-law's son Bakari, a 19-year-old who, according to his verbal résumé, had overseen a herd of 100 village cows. We made Mr. Gazelle the supervisor, and he opened his home to his new supervisee. It seemed like the perfect setup.

Both Mr. Gazelle and Bakari are Muslim, but neither of them knew how to pray. That is quite common here. It boggled my mind to see so many Muslim people who didn't know how to pray. If nothing else, you should at least know how to beseech your Creator, so Saidi offered to teach them both how to pray. They agreed. Saidi began giving them lessons each evening. He bought them prayer rugs, too. After that, Mr. Gazelle felt more comfortable coming to the mosque. He was too embarrassed before.

Despite his alleged experience, Bakari's work was subpar. The cows actually seemed to dislike him. They ran from him several times, but the climax was when our borrowed Ruvu bull came running from the bush, crashing through our compound wire fence. He ran all the way through the other side and didn't stop until he got back to Ruvu! I have no idea what Bakari did to upset that cow, but it must have been something major. Initially, he claimed they were running from a big leopard, but it didn't take long for him to retract his lie. A leopard in Jome? Unlikely!

I'm not sure when, but at some point, Mr. Gazelle and Bakari had stopped talking. One day, Mr. Gazelle brought a woven mat inside our compound and sat down. He didn't say a word at first. I guess he needed a minute to gather his thoughts. Then, out of nowhere, he started complaining about his wife cooking for Bakari but not for him. Then, one late night, he came to our bedroom window. With his voice shaking, he said, "My wife is inside Bakari's house. He screwed my wife."

Even though I did not understand Swahili, I could tell by the shaking of his voice and the stuttering of his words that the news was not good. I knew Bangi well enough to know that he only stuttered when he was worked up. The volume of his voice indicated that he did not want to conceal his discovery. It was a cry for help, any kind.

Saidi offered what Bangi needed, words of comfort. "Stay calm. Do not do anything you will feel sorry for later." Saidi then advised him to go back to the *banda* and stay away from Bakari's house. Saidi realized that in his emotional state, Bangi could do anything, maybe even a crime of passion. Saidi's voice was paternal and reassuring.

I wondered what we would do if the situation got out of hand. There was no 9-1-1 emergency response system in the bush for domestic violence. The next day, I reminded him not to assume, because such strong accusations in Islam require four witnesses. Bangi was still emotional, but he seemed to heed my words.

To be honest, I had already grown concerned about the long hours Mrs. Gazelle and Bakari spent together. He was often seen helping Mrs. Gazelle with her seaweed farm and farmland. We had a sesame farm and we paid locals to dig, 3 hectares of land (about 7.5 acres). Despite all the space, Mrs. Gazelle and Bakari always seemed to pick the same areas to dig. No way was that a coincidence. I tried to stay out of business that wasn't mine, but the time they spent together didn't feel right. It wasn't the Islamic way to go about things. After all, prevention is the best medicine. Eventually, we let Bakari go because Mr. Gazelle was not only our employee, but also our neighbor.

Within a week of Bakari's departure, Mrs. Gazelle decided to visit her mother, who just happened to live in the village next to Bakari's. At the same time, Mr. Gazelle informed us that his wife was pregnant and insisted it was his. Wishful thinking, perhaps? Either way, when Mr. Gazelle called his mother-in-law, his wife wasn't there. She hadn't been by at all. For three weeks, Mrs. Gazelle was "at her mother's house." Mr. Gazelle was left to care for his two young daughters alone. "She wants me to lose my job," he said. It was such a stressful time for him.

Mrs. Gazelle returned ill. "Female problems," they told us. We weren't sure what that meant, but we offered to take her to the hospital in town. She refused. After everything that had happened, Mr. Gazelle decided to divorce his wife. He married another wife during the three-month waiting period, which is the length of time a Muslim couple is supposed to wait before they finalize their divorce. Things would have been final, but Mrs. Gazelle's family begged him not to leave. Mr. and Mrs. Gazelle had just built a new house and had a successful cashew farm. The family didn't want the stress of dividing the assets. Since then, Mr. Gazelle has been balancing two wives.

With Bakari gone, we were desperate for another animal caretaker. Since Sijoli was still house-sitting, we asked him if he wanted to take care of the cows, goats and sheep. He agreed and became a salaried employee. But, again, Sijoli was true to his name. He did not care if the cows had water and would not walk with them to the river like other caretakers did. He told us taking care of the goats, sheep and cows was too much. We reduced the scope of his job by hiring Shuari from Ruvu to take care of the sheep and goats. Everyone's salary was adjusted accordingly.

If we could not get Sijoli to take the animals to the water, the water would have to come to the animals. We gave Mr. Gazelle, Shuari and Sijoli the daily responsibility of bringing three 20-liter buckets of water each. They shared the Jome bicycle. It would have worked well, but Sijoli kept getting flat tires without repairing them. He truly did not care.

We had a total of five cows, two bulls and three heifers. Two were pregnant. As much as we didn't want to, we decided to sell the cows because of their demanding daily water consumption, which was not conducive for our environment. Sijoli was out of a job—again. We hired people from the Sukuma tribe to walk our cows the 40 kilometers to their new home.

Shurai turned out to be a reliable worker. He did an excellent job caring for the goats and sheep. He also lived in Ruvu, so we did not have to house him. He was the perfect worker, almost. The only problem was that he spent long hours at Mr. Gazelle's home. With Mrs. Gazelle being there alone so frequently, we didn't want to risk any more love triangles. After about four months, Shurai took his salary and left for Dar. He never officially quit. He just left. He hasn't been seen in Jome or Ruvu since.

With so many people quitting without notice, Saidi and I started to question ourselves as bosses. Were we running people off? Then we met other people who assured us they had the same issue. It seems unskilled workers have trouble working long term. They get so used to working just enough for their immediate needs. If they have enough to get them through the week, they do not bother showing up anymore.

Even though Sijoli was no longer employed, he married and stayed in Jome. Mrs. Gazelle #1 found his wife for him. She had been living in Lindi town, selling fish on the streets. Sijoli had no other close family nearby. His parents died when he was young, and he lost his twin brother to a crocodile attack. We were all he had, so we invited him, again, to work for us as Shurai's replacement. He agreed. He worked for about a year before he quit and moved from his home in Jome. We heard he eventually landed a job taking care of cows in Ruvu. He walks them to the river, something he never did for us.

With Sijoli gone again, we decided against hiring anyone else for the goats and sheep. Mr. Gazelle agreed to open and lock up their *bandas* each day. We increased his salary to compensate for this 30-minute job. We hired out water fetching when needed. As much as we needed help in Jome, it was hard to find reliable workers who didn't abruptly quit for one reason or another. We agreed to rely on Mr. Gazelle for what we could and hire out the rest on an as-needed basis. Of course, not having as much help around has its consequences. One day, the sheep did not return, apparently the victims of four-legged or two-legged opportunists.

Even though we didn't have as much help as we originally planned, we did have Mr. Gazelle. Once he took on a second wife, he had to begin a juggling act that involved traveling back and forth between both wives. As you can imagine, it wasn't an easy task, so it didn't take long for him to move his second wife to Jome. She moved into Bakari's old house.

There was obvious, anticipated tension between the two wives. It was made worse by Sijoli's instigating wife. She would go between the two passing little bits of information back and forth. Sijoli being Sijoli, he ignored the whole situation. It didn't cause too many issues though. Mr. Gazelle seemed to trust his new wife, and it would be difficult for Mrs. Gazelle's #1 to earn back his trust.

Now Mr. Gazelle's salary was divided between two households. It was a lot to handle emotionally and financially. Eventually, the newer wife moved back to her home village of Kitomanga to farm. She was pregnant at the time. Mr. Gazelle followed. He told us he was going to farm and would be back in five days, but he knew he was leaving for good. As expected, he didn't come back.

We heard later that Mr. Gazelle's father-in-law in Kitomanga asked why he left a good job working for a *mzungu*. We wanted to know why he left with our keys, Jome mobile and a $185 debt he owed us. Upon our request, someone returned our phone and keys. The money was a 40-month loan for corrugated roof sheets he bought for the house he built for his Ruvu family. The money was being deducted from his salary each month, but he left 20 months before the loan was to be paid. More important, he also left his young daughters and pregnant first wife.

After we lost Mr. Gazelle, we were forced to return to the hunt for another helper. Saidi and I had already decided the next helper would be from outside the area. We felt we had exhausted the local pool. Hamisi suggested bringing in the Maasai, but I didn't like that idea. I have nothing against them. I know they are hired often as security in establishments frequented by tourists. In fact, they have a reputation for being good security guards, and tourists love to see them dressed in their native attire. The only problem was that I wanted a Muslim. I thought it was important because it would mean we would have similar cultures, especially diet. I also did not want to invite alcohol use to Jome. Given my conditions, Hamisi suggested Ali, a man from his home village.

We took care of the goats ourselves until Ali and his family arrived. It was quiet without Mr. Gazelle. It was different, but I enjoyed the time that was freed up from addressing the drama brought on by our helpers. We even burned the grass *banda* that had housed the helpers. Though we were happy to have peace, we were not happy that Mzee Ally and his wife were living 500 meters from us alone. Our other two local homes were vacant. We needed someone onsite for him.

Being from another tribe and village, Ali was initially apprehensive when he arrived, especially around the dogs. I couldn't put my finger on it, but there was something different about him and his wife. Then I learned they had finished primary school. They could both read and write. Sijoli and Mr. Gazelle never had a day of schooling in their lives. Not that schooling is everything, but there seems to be a certain level of professionalism and polish that people who have been to school have.

Ali's arrival brought life back to Jome. He had two daughters, ages six and four. He immediately got to work on his security guard *banda*. His wife planted flowers outside their home. His clothes were laundered every day as long as there was water to do so. There were new improvements to his home and our compound popping up on a daily basis.

Ali came to us from a village near Masasi. Like James, he had to adjust to life on the ocean. He wasn't used to being so close to the water, and his daughters couldn't swim. I was worried at first because he moved his family to Jome sight unseen. I wondered if they would like it. But I guess, like my moving to Tanzania, when it is time for a change, it is time for a change. He obviously trusted Hamisi, so he was willing to step out on faith. I feel so indebted to Hamisi for bringing us Ali and his family. Jome has definitely changed for the better.

With every live-in helper we've hired, I've wondered, is this the one that can help me in my old age? Is this the one that will make it possible for me to remain in Jome if Saidi precedes me? It is too early to say, but just maybe.

CHAPTER 14

ON SAFARI

Many *mzungu*s associate the word safari with an exciting drive through a game reserve park. I know I used to. Safari is actually a Swahili word that means "journey." Getting from one place to another in rural Tanzania is always a journey thanks to the condition of the roads.

Roads may seem like simple paths, but they are so much more. Roads are connections. They connect villages, districts, regions, countries and people. Likewise, the absence of good roads cuts people off from quality healthcare, commerce, education, power and water. My village was abandoned by the government decades ago. After the colonists left, ports closed, sisal industrial farmers left and the people of this area were abandoned. With no more money to be made off the area, the government lost interest.

With no good roads connecting Lindi district to the commercial capital of Dar, businesses left. Periodically, politicians promised development in the south. Contractors came and went, and with that the dreams of progress. In a country where every international NGO seems to have a strong presence, few can be seen in Lindi. The well-meaning expat *mzungu*s prefer to live their privileged existence in the cooler, more developed north. Few go south to stay.

In the midst of heavy rain, traveling south by road can be a real adventure—and by "adventure" I mean "challenge." It used to take days to travel between Dar and Lindi. Yet, a few more kilometers of tarmac are laid each year, giving hope to weary travelers. My first trip to Lindi required us to travel a 60-kilometer stretch of unpaved road. We left Dar about 7 AM and didn't arrive until 6 PM. It is only 460 kilometers, but it was the rainy season. Extended travel times were to be expected. We delayed our trip, trying to gauge the road and get updates from both Dar and Lindi. We wanted to go at the best possible time to minimize our hassle.

Despite all our planning, it was still the rainy season in rural Tanzania. We were bound to get stuck somewhere. Every time we got past a bad spot, we would end up in another. We had a Land Cruiser. It got around pretty well in the muddy conditions, but the trucks would get stuck and block the road. We would spend hours waiting for them to be dug out. We were fortunate that when we got a nail in our tire, we had just reached the paved road.

Of all our trips along the shoddy rural roads, we only turned back once. I will never forget that day. We had traveled two hours north toward Dar and were almost to the unpaved road. Then we were told that a horrible backup had left 300 vehicles on the road overnight. Opportunist boys tried to point out an alternate way, but we graciously declined their offer. Many have profited from the bad road, selling fried fish and drinks to weary travelers. We decided to drive to Mtwara so we could fly to Dar the next day. With Dar having the only real international airport in Tanzania, I now know it is wise to pad on a few days to assure an on-time arrival.

Three years after I moved to Lindi, my daughter and grandson visited. I had a great itinerary. We planned to visit Selous National Park and go on a game safari before heading to Jome. After our little tourist adventure, we got word that the road to Lindi was impassable. No buses were seen on either end of that 60-kilometer segment of so-called road. I love to stick to a well-thought-out plan, but I had experienced the wrath of that trip. I didn't want to chance it.

I recall one instance where we sat two hours in one place, then four hours in another—the latter being night, hot, humid and mosquito infested. In each case, we were stuck behind a line of buses, cars and trucks that were waiting for fully loaded semi-trucks to be dug out of foot-deep mud. It took 8.5 hours to travel the full 60-kilometer distance. Not wanting to repeat that experience with my daughter and grandson in tow or to be stuck in the bush without *mzungu* amenities, we returned to Dar and spent two days in a beachside resort before attempting the trip again. A few hours of sun can change the travel conditions drastically. It was still a soupy muddy mess, but we made it.

With each subsequent excursion, we are happy to see the progress being made between Dar and Lindi. It is almost all tarmac now, and it only took five years to pave 60 kilometers of road! We are also happy to see the development in Lindi and the increase in commerce and investment.

However, there are some real safety issues that need addressing, including an improved emergency response system. On the way to Lindi town, we saw four broken down trucks on a hill. On the way back, we saw two heavy-load trucks that were badly damaged. Then, we came across a fatal bus accident. Eleven dead. I am guessing there are at least 30 buses traveling fully loaded in each direction with passengers between Dar and Lindi. And mixed in with them are many heavy trucks. They whiz through villages, narrowly avoiding goats and cows. The road is one lane in each direction with no physical barrier between the two. Speed is often excessive for the conditions, but time is money for these land ships carrying people and goods down the African coast. Progress comes at a price. I can't help but wonder, if anything happens to us on this road, will we even have a chance of survival?

Though the roads are slowly getting better, most people still have no transportation. It is one reason Tanzania has a 529 maternal mortality per 100,000 pregnancies in contrast to the U.S., which has about 7 per 100,000. Foot is the primary method of transportation, followed by bicycle.

During those first trips to what would become my new home, Saidi would point to dirt paths worn down by pedestrians and bicycle traffic. He explained which paths led where. I am glad to see that, after four years of living in Jome, I now see Ruvu villagers with motorcycles.

Motorcycles are affordable and can reach areas that *daladalas* and cars would not dare to go. Many owners use them as taxis. Saidi and I have tossed around the idea of buying a motorcycle as backup transportation. It would be cost effective and would also cut out passengers waving us down for a lift. We're not quite ready for one, but maybe one day. It seems as something else takes priority in our monthly budget.

We try to be sympathetic to those who must travel long distances by foot, but our compassion comes at a price. We have had items stolen from our back seat. There is also the issue of smell and cargo. On our way back from Jome to Lindi, Saidi spotted women selling large fish on the road. He made a U-turn to buy a red snapper. The women then asked for a ride back to Lindi. It wasn't that we didn't want to help, but she had raw fish with her. The smell would have been unbearable. Lucky for us, they took a taxi instead. Saidi is finicky about odors in the car.

Have you ever seen the movie My Big Fat Greek Wedding? The father in it uses Windex for everything, even claims it cures acne. Well, Saidi is the same way, but instead of Windex, it is Expel (a strong mosquito repellant). One time, the car reeked after we took a bunch of *fundis* to Lindi. Saidi pulled over and made everyone look under their shoes to make sure they hadn't stepped in anything. After reaching home, Saidi had a party with the Expel. He fumigated the entire car.

Worse than the smell is the coughing. One day, a man waited at a location he knew we would pass; people from our village are good at recognizing our tire tracks. On our way back from Jome to Lindi, sure enough, he waved us down. The last thing we wanted was for someone to think we were snooty, so we gave him a ride. From the moment he got in the car, he was coughing like crazy. I whispered to Saidi, "He probably has TB." I opened the car windows and stayed quiet. Saidi finally asked him why he was going to Lindi. "For a TB appointment," he told us.

It may seem like the cities would be better. They aren't. Not by much anyway. Dar traffic is horrific even on a sunny weekday. I am amazed at how Saidi can navigate our SUV through the narrow streets during rush hour. There are busy intersections that have no working traffic lights. The street signs are crazy. I can not make sense of them. Drivers go through red lights, drive in the opposite direction down one-ways, and happily make illegal U-turns. I have asked Saidi repeatedly to explain the rules, but I cannot make sense of his answer either.

Attempting to improve the situation, traffic officers occasionally direct traffic at busy intersections, but I actually think they make matters worse. From a distance, they can't even be seen. Why can't the lights be programmed to direct traffic based on traffic patterns? That's the most logical solution. Instead, they sporadically place traffic officers everywhere except where they are needed the most: near the busy *daladala* stands.

These city mass transport buses will boldly break all laws to beat their competitors to a potential customer. There are two things that can make this intolerable situation worse: the motorcade of the president or other dignitaries, and rain. Dar's infrastructure is so poor that even a little rain creates deep puddles at the busiest of intersections.

Fortunately, rain is more of a blessing than curse in water-starved Lindi.

One day, we got stuck in Mchinga while waiting for the salt water to recede yet again. The weather was good and we were not fasting, so it wasn't that bad. Passing Mchinga to return home requires knowledge of the tide. Mchinga 2 is the first village off the tarmac. It is the entry point to six different villages, including Ruvu. At high tide, only a person who does not care about the devastating effect of salt water on their vehicle would drive through. We turned off the car and watched people roll up their pants to carry their bicycles across. At times like this, a vehicle is actually a disadvantage. The *daladalas* disembarked weary passengers prematurely to avoid the corrosive effect of the salt water. Even a customer-hungry *daladala* driver wouldn't risk it.

In town, the car taxi is becoming obsolete. They have been re-placed by motorcycles and *bajajis* (also known as rickshaws). Transport within town costs 1,000 TZS (about $0.60) for a motorcy-cle taxi and 1,500 TZS for a *bajaji*. This three-wheeled, fuel-efficient vehicle first got its fame in India, but now they are a fixture in Tanza-nia. Initially, the automobile taxi drivers were not happy—they couldn't possibly compete with the prices—but many of them adapted. They traded their cars in to join the *bajaji* revolution.

On any given day, corners near bus stands and markets are full of motorcycle and *bajaji* taxis competing for your fare. Periodically, the embassies of *mzungu* expats send out safety reminders to encourage residents to avoid *daladalas* and *bajajis*. Passengers on *daladalas* are easi-ly robbed because of the large crowds and limited space. By the look of things, most take their chances.

CHAPTER 15

FOUR-LEGGED FRIENDS AND FOES

O ne morning, Saidi decided to look over the goats and sheep as they exited their *bandas*. Sijoli was still working with us at this point, but he was unreliable. Saidi saw one of the goats pass by and noticed her rear end looked like a baboon's. Something black was protruding from it. He thought maybe she ate a plastic bag like our crazy dog, Jiwe, did when he was a little younger. Saidi told Sijoli to leave the goat behind while he called our animal doctor. The doctor said he would come immediately by bicycle, a 18-kilometer ride on a rough road.

Saidi suggested he take a motorcycle taxi at our expense. Amazingly, he arrived within 30 minutes. (Too bad humans here cannot get that kind of service.) Initially, based on the phone conversation, the doctor thought it was biting flies, a simple enough problem to remedy. Unfortunately, it wasn't biting flies.

The protruding item turned out to be an ear. Our doctor pulled out a dead, fully developed fetus. Apparently it got stuck during delivery and died. Saidi and the doctor buried it. Saidi praised the doctor for arriving as quickly as a *mzungu*, a comparison that many Tanzanians are happy to hear. The so-called, government-appointed animal doctor joked that he was from Chicago. I jokingly told him there were no goats or cows wandering the streets of Chicago. It became our running joke with him. We even referred to him as our Chicago doctor. He said the residual (placenta) would expel itself. True to his name, "I do not care" still had no idea what happened 24 hours later.

We hated to see our animals lose their offspring. They are just as important to us as the parents. We love them all. Saidi and I try to keep an eye on our animals, but we are used to our sheep and goats returning home on their own in the evening. One day, it got to be 6:00 PM and none of them had arrived yet. All five sheep and thirteen goats were missing. If they delayed much longer, they would surely have to sleep in the bush as they do not navigate well in the dark. Saidi decided to look for them.

He took his machete, two-way radio, pistol, flashlight and our two dogs. I was left with the cat and the other two-way. I paced from window to window to see if I could spot their return, making sure to keep the two-way nearby. Saidi and the dogs headed north, armed for whatever was ahead. About 60 meters into the search, the dogs stopped and their ears perked up. Amazingly, they circled around to the north side of the immobilized herd, driving them south to the house.

The goats and sheep scattered home, a chaotic scene. The sheep outran the goats. They were so distressed by the dogs that they all ran into the same *banda*. Rather than separate them, Saidi closed them all up together. They were a little more vocal that night as they tried to stake out their spot. Disturbed by all the commotion, the dogs barked most of the night. I admit, I am not really a dog person, but these two mutts are priceless.

On really hot days, Saidi and I sit inside the compound wall to enjoy the breeze. We had just accepted the idea that we lost one of our goats (either in a trap, consumed by a predator or stolen). A few hours earlier, one group of goats returned a little later than the other.

Saidi wondered why the second group was late. They usually return a couple times a day for water and then stick close to home in the evening. That's when we let the babies out. But that day, when the second group returned, they didn't get a last drink of water like usual. Instead, they stopped at our compound gate, looked at Saidi and cried.

They wouldn't move from that spot. Saidi did a head count and saw that one young goat was missing. We called our neighbor, Mrs. Gazelle #1. She lived about one mile south of us. She said she had heard something in the bush and would go look. Saidi decided to head north, taking a two-way radio with him. He found nothing, so he locked up the other goats and sheep.

Later, as we sat in the compound close to sunset, we saw Mrs. Gazelle's girls approaching. They had the goat! Their mom found it in a trap and cut it loose. I gave them some chocolate bars as a thank you.

Another day, our neighbor thought she was doing us a favor and opened the goat/sheep compound. She didn't realize how challenging it would be to get the babies back in the nursery. While she pondered a strategy, the goats escaped followed shortly after by the sheep. The sheep lost sight of their navigators. The goats returned, but the sheep were nowhere to be found. We hoped it was possible for them to still come back, assuming some unscrupulous person did not slaughter them and sell the meat.

However, as the days passed, so did our hope. We offered a reward of $30, and people actually searched the bush for a few days. Nothing was returned though. Eventually, we had to accept the idea that, like most people here, we would have to stick with the more-maintenance-free goats. Besides, the only reason we decided to invest in sheep is because I enjoyed lamb more than goat. Saidi recalled that his father also had sheep in Jome at one point, so he was happy to comply with my request. Over time, my tastes changed and I grew to appreciate the taste of goat.

The first two sheep we ever had were named Walter and Rebecca. From the beginning, they were a handful. Looking back, their presence may have contributed to Bima's decision to leave so abruptly. Several evenings a week, we followed Walter and Rebecca's footprints. They would eat until they were full and forget to come home. We tracked them to the beach north of the house, sleeping in the sand. Other times, when the tide came in, they did not know how to navigate past the rising water.

I still have a vision of us returning from town to find Bima transporting a sleeping Rebecca and Walter in a basket on the back of his bicycle. Things did improve, however, especially when they stayed with their cousins the goats. Our attempts to hire people to stick with the herd were futile as the animals often went deep into the forest. The herd of sheep grew slowly, nowhere near as fast as the goats. While goats typically birth multiples, sheep are known only for single births. I began to understand why few villagers invested in sheep.

Given their aloofness, we considered putting electronic tracking devices on the sheep. The best we could do was tag their ears, but that still relied on a person of conscious to return the lost sheep. Sadly, that is rare. To be fair, one seaweed farmer did abandon her work once to report seeing a sheep we bought for Eid-ul-Adha in the mangrove forest. Pleased by her honesty and efforts, we gave her a small financial reward and invited her to a glass of juice, hoping to also send the message that honesty pays. Unfortunately, the value of a herd of sheep is often too tempting for those who live on less than two dollars a day.

With our conscious decision to reduce the help, we decided not to continue to keep sheep in Jome. After our sheep went missing, we didn't bother buying any more. A few weeks later, two full-grown goats went missing as well. Two-legged foes most likely.

We do miss our sheep though. Compared to goats, they are, as Saidi says, polite. Yet, sheep can hold their own against goats. When the male goats challenged Walter to a fight, the goats were the ones we were worried about. Sheep's heads are much harder than goats.

Like young children, they soon forget their squabbles and walk off together as friends.

Still, the sheep's politeness was their demise. While out grazing in the bush with the hyper goats, sheep are often left behind by their navigators. By the time they look up from their methodical, steady eating, the goats have already vanished. It is their politeness that leads Saidi to want to buy more sheep. I am quick to remind him of Walter and Rebecca.

After abandoning the sheep plan, we took solace in the productivity of the goats. We had invested in a male goat that was twice the cost of most others. When we bought him, he was still a teenager, but the owner pointed out his huge father. It did not take long to see that our investment paid off as he towered over the other goats in no time.

Our Chicago doctor made a house call and neutered all our other adult male goats. Big Man, as we soon began calling him, produced male goats that were his equal, and the female offspring were large as well. People were amazed at Big Man and, from a distance, thought he was a cow. After a while though, we knew it was time to reduce the male population. We bartered one male baby for a female. He ended up getting stolen from his new owner within 24 hours. More two-legged foes.

Once we had a whole family of Big Man-sized goats, we decided to barter Big Man for solar power services with Hamisi. He gave Big Man to his mother who, upon seeing him, said she would have to keep him tied so he would not get stolen. However, with goats' naturally high fertility rate, we decided to just wing it and not bother trying to confine them; we would live with the natural and unnatural attrition.

While away in town, we missed the birth of a baby girl. We thought a different mother-to-be would be next to deliver, so this one surprised us. An octopus fisherman from the village happened to see the goat and her new baby. Kindly, he carried the baby to our house with mom following close behind. Despite the fact that all the adults were tagged on their ears, we worried where they would give birth and whether or not we would be able to find them. Sometimes they forced themselves into our thatched beachside huts to birth (or to get out of the rain).

Goats are known for having multiples, so it wasn't much of a surprise when one of our mothers delivered triplets. Saidi remarked, "This mom is clever," because she stayed behind and did not go out to eat with the others. I know the last thing I wanted to do was eat when I was in labor; I wanted quite the opposite actually. We call her Triple Mom as she has given birth to triplets four times. However, each time, one of the three has died. In the first case, "I do not care" did not put all the babies in the nursery, so the young kid was trampled. In the second case, it was just a runt that could not compete for milk. It is sad to see a baby not make it, but goats seem to deliver every six to eight months. They are constantly producing new life.

If you are observant, it does not take long to see that animals have personality, too. My goodness, do they! Saidi was growing very tired of one young kid that we recently allowed to leave the nursery in the day time. In the evening, his twin brother and mother would go up the ramp into the *banda* with no problem, but not him.

The mother would stand at the door and refuse to let any other goats inside until her son was in the *banda*. Each evening, we (mostly Saidi) chased the goat around in a muddy goat compound during the rainy season. Eventually, we tried trapping him with a fishnet. No luck. We both looked at each other and sighed in unison, "He is too young to eat." As it turns out, he was just a slow learner. In about two weeks, he was going up the ramp like a pro.

One evening, Saidi heard a noise near the gate outside. He found a baby goat covered in amniotic fluid and protective membrane. Saidi wondered where the mom had gone. Saidi then saw the second one popping his head out as the mom walked to a shaded area. We carried the firstborn over to the same location. The newborns struggled to stand for the first 30 minutes. The mom seemed hesitant to go to her *banda*, so we listened to see if there was a third one somewhere. We let them rest for about an hour before carrying them, followed by the mom, to their compound.

I thought it was funny that one of the newborns kept following me around like I had milk for her; it had been 25 years since I did. I was happy for this mom. She was the same one that had a stillbirth back when "I do not care" was working for us.

We had too many "active" boys, so we bartered another for a female. The next day, we had invited two-legged guests. Goat was on the menu. I try not to get attached.

Our animals are not the only ones surrounding Jome. Once, I had a close encounter with something much more exotic. We were on the tarmac and noticed an animal on the road. "What is that? Is it a dog?" I asked. It looked too small to be a cow and too big to be a goat, the two most common animals you must avoid when driving. It was a cheetah. This took us by surprise because we were not near a national park. Then, it became obvious. We saw many goats in the area. The cheetah must have been on a hunt. Saidi and our passenger did not seem moved, but it was quite exciting for this *mzungu*.

Other random sightings are a little less pleasant. While waiting for the water to recede in Mchinga, I saw a man carrying a liver and another with a cow's hide draped across his shoulders. About 30 minutes earlier, we passed an accident in which three cows were hit by a truck. On the other side of the water, a car waited and the passengers were approached by men trying to sell what looked like the other half of the slaughtered cow.

Of course, they tried to sell to us, but it was questionable if the meet was *halal*. In other words, if the cow was killed by the truck, it wouldn't have been permissible to eat. If the cow was injured but then slaughtered while alive, it would have been Islamically acceptable. One of the would-be entrepreneurs said the cow had been sick. Another said they killed it Islamically after an accident. Umm, no thanks!

Slaughtering cows (and all animals) properly is important in Islam, especially on Eid. Once a year, Ruvu slaughters a cow for Eid-ul-Adha. The meat is used for what they call *dhikri*. At that time, Ruvu is flooded with its sons and daughters from Dar and other villages. People from Dar save all year for the event, renting two buses for their two-day visit. Ruvu's *dhikri* committee is chaired by the Ruvu cow manager. It is interesting that Ruvu, a fishing village, is now the owner of cows. Owning cows gives options. That's always a good thing.

Ruminants were not our only four-legged friends. From the first sighting of the ugly (rats in Lindi), we considered getting a cat. One day, Saidi came home with a burlap bag. "I have a gift," he said. Inside was a tiny kitten. We decided to name her Lindi after the town she came from.

For the first few days, we thought we lost her. We searched daily for the faint cries. We couldn't be certain, but it sounded like it was coming from outside. Finally, we found her wedged under a wooden closet.

She got used to her new home. But like most kittens, she found the mosquito net much more enticing. We ended up taking her to Jome to live with the *fundis*. We thought they would welcome the company, but they did not see her as a friend. They did not understand that when she slept on top of them, it was only because she had witnessed a big *kenge* (monitor lizard) eating her food and theirs. The *fundis* viewed her as competition for their fish, so they kicked her out. With the house almost finished, I decided to move her in.

Lindi is definitely a *mzungu* cat. She sleeps on a foam mattress bed in our room. She gets distressed when left alone. Still, a cat is a cat, and I give her credit for never allowing a rat in our home. She alerts us to any intruders, particular geckos, which she considers a delicacy. More importantly, she earned her keep at least once when Saidi found her fighting a venomous green mamba snake. We quickly learned to pay attention to Lindi.

Of all our Jome animals, Lindi was our first four-legged friend. We often jokingly remind her she is the senior of all the four-legged friends. However, her value is sometimes challenged when she goes into heat.

Our Chicago animal doctor does not have the skills to spay a female animal, so we're forced to tolerate her periodic, excruciating wailing. We feel for her and know she can do nothing to stop the explosive surge of hormones. When the urge hits her, she goes downstairs to be alone, only to return until the next wave.

Our second four-legged friend, Mchanga, arrived as a puppy. She had a sand-colored coat, hence the name Mchanga, which means "sand" in Swahili. We knew we needed a dog in the bush for protection, so we immediately began to look once the dog house was complete. We attempted to get a big breed police dog, but each deal mysteriously fell through. We were told the puppies died or the mother miscarried. That's OK. Mchanga, a mutt, was just fine.

She was a great warner, always barking at passersby, including the occasional hyena. However, it was obvious she was lonely. We knew we had to get her a friend. Why not? Saidi and I have each other. Mchanga needed a mate, too. We ended up buying her half-brother, six months her junior. We named him Jiwe, meaning "stone" in Swahili. Jiwe arrived as a puppy as well, and Mchanga made it clear she was his senior. She would bark at him any time he wandered off too far.

Jiwe was a digger from the beginning. As a puppy, he caused us to have to move our emergency set of keys that was buried in the dirt under a tree. An adventurous pup, it did not take long for him to begin to leave the compound at night, burrowing under the wired fence. Occasionally, Mchanga followed. Despite being the younger one, Jiwe was clearly the ring leader. He would steal, destroy and chew anything carelessly left in a 100-meter radius of the house. Frustrated, Saidi began to threaten to sell crazy Jiwe, but I assured him he would change with age.

Mchanga and Jiwe are a team. When predators visit, Mchanga guards the house as Jiwe pushs back the unwelcomed visitors. But during their late night follies, like clockwork, Jiwe would always return home first. Often, Mchanga would stay out until the following afternoon, sometimes returning with the goats. We grew concerned that she would get pregnant by a stray. We were not prepared for puppies. Jiwe was crudely neutered by our wannabe Chicago doctor. As busy as they were, our dogs gave us another reason to invest in a compound wall.

Our plan was to keep Jiwe and Mchanga confined during the day. It didn't work. Jiwe, our chewer, ate through the wire window and jumped out. Mchanga, on the other hand, wouldn't dare. Despite his destructive ways, it was Jiwe that seemed more disciplined, never jumping on us and only participating in the killing of a chicken if Mchanga was first to attack. It was Mchanga who, if given the opportunity, would invade the chicken house and eat all the eggs. They had very distinct personalities. It was interesting to watch.

Just like our helpers, our animals bring life to Jome. In different ways, they add value to our home. They keep us busy with their human-like personalities and give us food, protection and financial opportunities. What would Jome be without our four-legged friends? We are truly grateful for them all, even the ones we couldn't keep.

CHAPTER 16

OUR FLOWERS ON THE MOVE

From our first days in Jome, we knew we wanted to keep chickens. Besides the obvious dietary benefits, they are fun to have around. We would spend long hours just watching them scratch and peck. Like other animals, chickens have personalities. They mimic Pavlov's dogs perfectly. Every time I go outdoors with a metal tray, they come running, wondering what delicacies I have for them. They're hearty little guys, able to survive through rain and drought. Saidi began calling them our flowers because they seem to thrive in any season.

Though it was our decision to keep chickens in Jome, they were already here before we arrived. Actually, they were at Mr. Gazelle's house. The first two hens we physically brought to Jome were rescued from the market in Lindi. We introduced them to a rooster we'd been gifted, but another rooster quickly courted one of them. There was some fighting when we first put all the chickens together, but we were told that was their way of welcoming the newcomers.

One day, we found Mr. Gazelle's children waiting on the road for us with a bag of mangoes. They had some news: our rooster was impotent. Perhaps the mangoes were to soften the blow. After Saidi translated, I wondered how the children actually said it. What words had they used to communicate such a complex idea?

The local roosters were a bit too feisty. The fighting never died down, so we had to sell them. That left our impotent rooster with about 20 hens all to himself. But, of course, nothing happened. We needed to grow our numbers, so we agreed that Mr. Gazelle's family would sell our rooster and both families would buy another.

Fortunately, our wannabe Chicago doctor sold us Big Bird a few months later. At more than twice the price of other chickens, he has proven to be worth every schilling. Now almost all our chickens are descendants of Big Bird. He is a real patriarch.

With nothing more than a wired fence around the compound, the chickens were under constant attack. Clearly, we were not the only ones who loved chicken. One night, I was awakened by the sound of an attack. The dogs barked to alert us. After Saidi called Mr. Gazelle, who was sleeping outside our compound in our thatched hut, I went to the window to watch. "Two chickens are dead, and the predator ran off," Mr. Gazelle said. Ran off? Saidi thought that couldn't be true. Big Bird, our alpha rooster, had run out of the *banda* and was covering his head. Something was still inside.

Saidi went outside carrying the long steel pole he had used to kill a chicken egg-thieving monitor lizard several months earlier. I waited quietly, wondering what it could be. Finally, when it was safe, I went outside to get a closer look. There were three victims: a hen who had been sitting on her eggs, one of our up-and-coming smaller roosters and a small chicken.

When I saw the now-deceased predator, I wasn't sure what I was looking at. I searched for the English word to describe it. No luck. I later found out it is called a civet. People here say they like to kill chickens and take the heads only. I guess they do it for sport. Luckily, this one didn't get a chance to do that.

I always enjoy the proud stories of my bush warrior husband. He lights up like a child telling his favorite fairytale. "I made the first strike through the shoulder and pinned the animal down in the ban-da," he said proudly. "I told Mr. Gazelle to go inside and strike it to finish the job. He reluctantly did after being told several times to stop talking. It was time for action, not talk." His stories are always so live-ly. There may be a tinge of exaggeration here and there, but I do not mind. I love listening to him.

I also love our chickens, so much that the thought of eating them now bothers me. Though we do not eat much meat, I wanted to cook a traditional meal for Thanksgiving. With no turkey around, chicken was as close as I would get. As much as I like chicken, I found myself making excuses not to eat them. How could I? Our dear Big Bird had begun to eat from our hands. We were friends. You do not eat your friends. Besides, his meat is sure to be tough due to his age, strength and size. We ended up eating another rooster, one that had been ag-gravating our Big Bird.

With the impotent chicken replaced, our chicken *bandas* were get-ting crowded. Big Mama, one of our hens, had had enough. She decided to move into the workers' *banda*. All the chickens that hatched in that *banda* considered it home. We ended up with three generations of chickens in the worker's *banda*. Poor Mr. Gazelle never made the correlation between the chickens and the fleas in his bed. I guess he loves chickens as much as I do, because it never occurred to him that sleeping on the same mattress with a chicken and her eggs would be problematic.

Knowing the chickens needed a new home, we quickly finished the brick work on the new chicken house. Two sides of the chicken house shared a wall with the compound wall. Two sides had large screened windows. Instead of a thatched roof, they now had corru-gated metal roof sheets. The old wired door from our compound fence became their new full-sized door. When our animal doctor saw the house, he said, "That is not a chicken house; that is a poultry house."

Moving the chickens with their eggs and little ones was a noisy ordeal, but our flowers thrived after moving day. The younger ones are now confined within the compound due to the brick wall. Older ones occasionally fly over the wall. The biggest peril that remains seems to be birds of prey, but Big Bird gives a warning sound when any potential predatory bird flies overhead.

The flowers all go scrambling under trees, chairs and shrubs. Saidi then goes outside with his slingshot. Before the new house, eggs, chicks and even full-grown chickens were picked off by pythons, civets, monitor lizards, monkeys and maybe even people. Predators now have to be clever to disturb our precious flowers.

One day, I heard the peeps of a small chick from the kitchen window. When I investigated, I saw a young chick trying to stay afloat in a bucket of water someone had left outside. Quickly, I rescued the shivering chick, but he was so small and frail that I didn't think he would make it. When I tried to carry the chick to the chicken house, the mother attacked me, flying waist high! Lucky for her, I understood her motherly instinct. I backed away to let her know my intentions were pure.

The mother chicken spent the rest of the evening sitting on her cold, wet baby chick. The next day, it looked as strong as its siblings. A full recovery, or so I thought. I didn't see the chick anymore after that. The mother busied herself with her remaining chicks. I guess it wasn't meant to be. It is funny, in the States, calling someone a chicken is an insult. It means they are scared or weak. But chickens are a resilient lot. No matter what, they endure. No matter what, they thrive. I love that about them.

CHAPTER 17

THE FOUNDATION

I had successfully built a *mzungu* home, staffed it with helpers (of varying reliability) and filled it with an assortment of animals. But so what? None of that matters in the grand scheme of things. These are the questions that whirled around in my head. I didn't want to become complacent. I didn't want to be the kind of person who became satisfied with myself just because I left America for a "developing" country. So what? I have to do more. From the beginning of when I came to Africa, I've been a part of efforts to improve the healthcare in the region. Now that I called Tanzania my home, I felt I wanted to build a localized organization which would be self-sustaining and take on the role of funneling charitable contributions to address health, education and Muslim institutions.

It struck me how so many friends and acquaintances had responded to pictures and stories of my emergence into another culture. They obviously saw the contrast between their lives and those of people living on less than $2 per day. These people, some of whom were complete strangers and all of whom had no connection to Tanzania, were moved enough to send unsolicited donations for me to use for the villagers.

Encouraged by their generosity, Saidi and I decided to try to institutionalize this flow of sporadic philanthropy. We decided to register **Lindi Islamic Foundation of Tanzania** (LIFT), a volunteer faith-based organization.

After scratching out the organizational structure, framework, and governance model, I sat down and wrote the LIFT Meeting Rules:

1. Notify chairperson and secretary as soon as possible if you cannot attend.
2. Come prepared. Read and review agenda, any previous meeting minutes, and documents prior to meeting.
3. Arrive early and start on time.
4. Conduct one conversation at a time.
5. Avoid using mobiles, put them on silence.
6. Respond to the topic.
7. Be solution-minded: When you identify a problem, suggest a solution.
8. Be specific when identifying action items: What? Who? When?
9. Be prepared to take personal notes (bring paper and pen).
10. Bring your personal calendar for scheduling of future meetings and events.
11. Save non-agenda items for Round Table discussion or add to future meeting's agenda.
12. Ask: How can I help?
13. Observe time limits, and end the meeting as scheduled.

Rule #3 would be a toughie, I knew. Time is a negotiable resource. A common perception of people of color is that we are notoriously late. Some believe it is part of our DNA. Among older African Americans, we sometimes internally joke about CPT or Colored People Time.

As my circle of friends increased to include people from around the world, including Arabs, East Indians and Pakistanis, I realized that the lax outlook on time was not isolated to my African American brothers and sisters. In fact, it seems Europeans and Americans are the only ones with the "Time is money" worldview.

Of course, the ability to be on time is not in one's DNA. We all have the ability to be punctual if we believe it is important to do so. As a corporate America trained professional, I know this to be true. I vowed that my foundation would defy the stereotype.

That was before I realized just how hard it is to get people from a totally different culture to value the concept of being on time. Part of the problem is that you cannot simply translate time straight from English to Swahili. The Swahili day starts at 6:00 AM. It makes sense, I guess. The day starts at sunrise and ends at sunset. However, this means that if a meeting is scheduled at 10:00 AM, you would say in Swahili, Saa nne asubuhi, meaning "the 4th hour in the morning." I often wondered if I should set the clock in the office to Swahili time or *mzungu* time.

It was confusing at first, but I learned how to translate the time by adding and subtracting six depending on if it was morning or afternoon. Fortunately, English-speaking people understand *mzungu* time. That's the rule: *mzungu* time when speaking English, Swahili time when speaking Swahili. However, *mzungu* time has a double meaning; it also means LIFT meeting rule #3: BE ON TIME.

When it came to writing the constitution, I knew where to start. Thanks to people who assumed my mission in Lindi was to start a local NGO, I already had sample constitutions waiting in my inbox. Why reinvent the wheel? I used what I had as a template and filled in the particulars.

With a draft in hand, we went to the well-connected Hamisi. According to the government regulations, we needed 10 founding members and a board of directors. With Hamisi's assistance, we were able to file our application with the Tanzanian Ministry of Home Affairs in what their website said would be a four-day process. Seven months after the first board of directors meeting and five months after submitting our application, we were the first registered Muslim faith-based organization headquartered in Lindi.

I have no idea why the website said the process would only take four days. There was so much to do: several trips to Dar at our expense, email exchanges between the government lawyer investigating our application, meeting the requirement to establish a physical office, payment of the application fee, submission of CVs and pictures of all board directors, three iterations of letters of recommendation from the Lindi district commissioner, a letter of recommendation from the government-sponsored Muslim council, an investigation by internal security, a lot of patience and even a little pleading from our parliament representative.

Three months after registration approval, we had our first all-member meeting. My excitement quickly gave way to anger when I noticed that our presenter and most of the other board directors were late. Even the food was late. Did no one read meeting rule #3?

I calmed down when I saw that no one else cared we were off schedule. Overall, it went well and seemed professional. The members listened attentively to a PowerPoint presentation on LIFT's brief history, mission, vision, values and organizational structure, which included committee vacancies and committee descriptions.

By the end of the meeting, we had a list of volunteers for each of LIFT's committees. One week later, we had CVs for those seeking committee chair positions. I guess my insistence on punctuality sunk in. By the second committee chair meeting, most participants were already waiting for me outside the office by the time I arrived.

Initially, we targeted Ruvu for our philanthropic efforts. It only seemed natural. Even before we married, Saidi did what he could for the village. For example, he brought carpet for the mosque from Dar during one of his visits. For a few years, we had already been funneling money into the village through individual donations from friends, collective donations from my mosque in Michigan and our personal donations. We usually used the money to buy things like food and supplies for the village, but sometimes we gave it to elderly individuals in need.

We had a soft spot for children. They are the future. We always did what we could for them. Before moving to Jome, we had a custom wheelchair made for Hasan, a 12-year-old lame boy. He had never been able to attend school before that. Thankful for the gift, he approached me one day and handed me a plastic bag. I found inside the results of his tests: 100% on English. This was all before the organization, but we continued to follow suit after LIFT was established.

Most of our donations are from people looking to gain nothing other than the pleasure of God. The largest gift was our attempt to drill for water. That didn't work out, but we were able to build an Islamic school for Ruvu, pay salaries for the *madrasa* teachers, sponsor daily *iftar* programs, lay tiles in the mosque and install solar lighting and a speaker system. We were overcome with joy when we first heard from Jome the *muezzin* call the *adhan* in Ruvu.

Not all gifts come from Muslims. When people see the level of need here, they are often moved to help regardless of their religious beliefs. An ex-colleague, non-Muslim, bought English books for all students at Ruvu Primary School. Before that, the whole class shared one book. Another friend, also non-Muslim, sent money to help pay for Hasan's school uniform and school supplies. LIFT is open to working with anyone who wants to help. We appreciate the generosity of all our donors.

Like all charities, we have our challenges. The biggest is funding. As helpful as our overseas donors are, we can't rely on them exclusively. To keep things going, we need a steady flow of money. But in the meantime, there is much work to do to build capacity among the volunteers. I am hopeful the foundation can make a difference in the Lindi region through enhancements in education, food security, health, water and sanitation, and spiritual growth. It is my hope that I can reduce my footprint in the organization so people will no longer refer to it as the foundation started by Mama *Mzungu*. This foundation is for the people of Lindi. I want them to take ownership of it.

CHAPTER 18

TWO-LEGGED NEIGHBORS

Because I had made a custom of bringing candy to the children of Ruvu, they continued to expect it after I stopped. One day on a trip to check on the progress in Jome, the children noticed our car and immediately began to follow. I tried to motion that I had nothing for them, but they followed us for three kilometers.

Sometimes while driving through villages, Saidi would stop to talk to some of the village or mosque elders. I would learn later that much of the conversations were about small projects or requests.

"Our mosque needs solar lights."

"We need a few bags of cement to finish the toilet at the mosque."

"The speaker for the mosque no longer works." Saidi would exit the car and engage in conversation, seemingly unaware of my predicament. As this scene repeated, I began to understand that he considered this a better solution than men crowding around the car talking about their problems while scanning the interior of our car with a crowd of children listening on. Besides, Saidi being their junior, it was more polite, respectful and engaging on Saidi's part.

Nevertheless, I had no peace. I tried to relax and read a book, but the children crowded around and starred at me. I wondered, is this what life will be like in Jome, everyone staring like I'm part of some exhibit?

My skin color was lighter than most. Aesthetically, I knew I would always stand out, but I didn't want to feel like I stood out. I felt guilty—and selfish. This was Saidi's homeland. Why couldn't I just accept that I was different and not take everything personally? We had both sacrificed our jobs and familiar surroundings to be with each other. No turning back now.

Originally, things looked hopeful. Everyone seemed so happy to see Saidi, their returning son. They were eager to help us get established. Fifty men from Ruvu made the road from the Ruvu junction to Jome. It only took them three days. Jome was now reachable by car. And when the chassis broke on the water delivery truck on its way to Jome, the people of Ruvu were right there to help us. Bucket by bucket, they began transporting the water on foot just after dawn. Nearly 6,000 liters and 280 buckets later, the job was complete. It was *Ramadan.* They were all fasting. I gave them tea and dates at sundown. It was the least I could do.

Because Jome is so remote, there aren't many people around. Mr. Gazelle was our nearest neighbor. He lived outside the inner village. Before he became one of our Jome helpers, we knew him as the guy with the adorable daughters. I kept candy in the car just for them. It was cute to watch their excitement the first few times they rode in our car. Cars are a rarity in Ruvu. Even adults need help opening the door sometimes.

One day, while heading to Jome to check on the construction, we were waved down by some men. They told us one of Mr. Gazelle's daughters was very ill. I'm not sure how long they had been waiting for us to drive by, but it could have been days. The daughter, maybe

10 years old or so, had signs of jaundice. Wanting to be good neighbors, we dropped them at Mr. Gazelle's sister's house in Lindi town and gave Mr. Gazelle about $25.

He did not want go to the hospital, not until Monday anyway. That's when the *mzungu* doctors are in at regional hospitals. When we returned to Jome that weekend, his wife was waiting on the road to ask us the prognosis. We didn't have anything to report but tried to ease her obvious concern. We told her that her husband had our phone number and would call when he needed or knew anything.

Once her diagnosis was complete, we visited the young girl and her family. The paperwork only indicated jaundice, but there were many medications prescribed: two different types of antibiotics, quinine (for malaria—yuk!), deworming medicine, mild pain medicine and anti-nausea medicine. We told them to make sure she took it all, drank plenty of fluids and took the medication with food. Before leaving, we gave them a little money for bottled water. That was the beginning of a four year whirl-wind relationship.

As the house was being built, we took small vacations to the land that would soon be our permanent home. It was a relaxing way for us to get some R&R. One day, after grabbing my Jome survival kit, (i.e., light lunch and thermos), I stepped inside our *banda*. Immediately, I noticed some cassava on a garbage pail cover. Strange. I also heard a noise coming from above. I looked up and saw a monkey looking down at me! Quickly and without theatrics, I left. I told Saidi, "Someone has been in our *banda*, and there is a monkey there."

James, who was standing nearby, said, "Oh, Rashidi caught it and thought Mama [me] would like it." Why they thought I would like a monkey is beyond me, but I did find it amusing—until the monkey defecated. He had to go. James removed him and tied him up outside. He said Rashidi would release him when he returned from the village.

Three days later, the monkey was still there. As it turns out, Rashidi loved the little guy. They had become close. To Rashidi's credit,

I did notice the monkey seemed more mild mannered, less disturbed by my presence. Still, I thought it was best he let it go. Sitting at the end of a rope in the hot sun is no life for a wild animal. He needed his freedom, and I was scared he might find himself in an altercation with an even wilder animal. Plus, locals find them a menace, especially farmers.

We began to shrug our shoulders at the 1,000,000 TZS land deal, recognizing it was against our interest to receive a gift from a wealthy land prospector. We also tried not to make a big deal out of the cement caper. We didn't want to judge everyone based on the actions of a few. We tried our best to stay positive at all times, but there were four incidents that were, to say the least, very disappointing. They made me question our approach to uplifting the community. They involved educating the youth, protecting and feeding children, and fulfilling donors' Islamic obligation.

First: As children and education are both close to my heart, I was overjoyed to hear that one of my friends decided to sponsor a Ruvu child for six years of private post-primary school. We set a criteria based on academic success at both the government primary school and the part-time Islamic school. After consulting the teachers of both schools, a worthy student named Khatib was selected.

One year later, Saidi and I decided to sponsor a child ourselves, a girl. I wanted the process to be more transparent this time, so I selected a date and invited all girls who had passed primary school to come to Jome for a small interview. We made posters, prepared gifts for all the participants and invited the teachers of the Islamic school to participate in the selection process.

When the day arrived, I waited and waited. Not one student arrived, not even the teachers. If even one student had shown up, we would have gladly awarded the sponsorship to her. I was beginning to learn how suspicion was poisoning the people.

When the village heard about our plan to sponsor a female student, they automatically assumed Khatib's sister would win. Unfortunately, at an event in a nearby village, she mysteriously died after eating a meal. Many people assumed she was the victim of envy—and poison. How could two children from the same family be recipients of such a rare gift like private education at an Islamic secondary boarding school? I guess no one wanted to be the next victim, so they all stayed home. Not even the *imam*'s daughter came. That really surprised us.

There were some who actually blamed the *imam* for the girl's death, but that I refuse to believe; it was quite unsubstantiated. However, a few days after the scheduled interviews, the *imam* called. "What about my daughter?" he asked. Frustrated, Saidi told him that the time had passed and pointed out that he, the *imam*, had been the one to post the announcements.

The second incident was particularly disturbing and still bothers me to this day. It involved a primary school child who was repeatedly raped by her stepfather. The mother actually caught her husband in the act. She screamed, cried and reacted like any mother would. A male relative escorted the abuser to Lindi.

We heard the story first from one of the elders who was doing a small job for us. He seemed unmoved by the whole thing and said the families were actually taking up donations to get him released from jail. Released? Why? Did they not see this as a terrible violation? To make matters worse, the offender went on to justify the act by saying the young girl had already been "opened." I was absolutely appalled.

Three months later, and after a 300,000 TZS (or a mere $180) payment, the man was home under the same roof with his wife and stepdaughter. It disgusts me to see a perpetrator—a teacher at Ruvu's *madrasa* no less— living among vulnerable children. And Ruvu is not alone in their shame. We have heard countless TV evangelists crying in front of their pulpits, asking their flock for forgiveness. The Catholic Church is still wrestling with how to heal after finally acknowledging a painful era of abuse and cover up. I felt so hopeless.

How could I continue to help a community that would not even protect its most vulnerable and valuable assets? I wondered what the mother thought. Just months earlier, she was screaming with outrage. Now she had moved this man back into her home with her daughter. How can a mother justify such a decision? What thought process must she go through to come to that conclusion? I was baffled. Even more shameful were those who asked him to return to teaching. Thankfully, he declined.

The third incident involved a recurring donation that was later assumed by a friend I met on Facebook. Every month, we bought flour, sugar and soy for Ruvu Primary School. The children would carry water and firewood to earn porridge each day. Mr. Gazelle's children were a good resource to gauge how the program was going. I would ask, "How is school? Did you have porridge today? What about yesterday?"

One day, we found out porridge was no longer being prepared, because the pot had cracked. The headmaster of the school asked the village if he could borrow one of the village pots. (Ruvu owns several large pots that are used primarily to feed guests for Ruvu's annual Eid-ul-Adha *dhikri*.) The village agreed to rent the pot to the school for the porridge program to feed their own children. The headmaster happily declined, and the teachers all contributed to buy a replacement pot.

Things were going well until a school village committee chair decided to taste the porridge. He complained that it did not have enough sugar. The headmaster responded, "If you do not think it has enough sugar for your child, then you can give a little sugar to your child for his portion."

Outraged, the committee chair left and never returned again. He also unapologetically refused to send his daughter, who had passed primary school exams, to secondary school. To pass school exams is a wonderful accomplishment—many students fail, especially girls—but instead of encouraging his daughter to further her education, he refused to pay her school fees. Yet, he bragged about having rental houses in Dar. When the porridge program ended due to a lack of requested reporting from the school, no one asked what happened.

These are the types of events that led to the gradual deterioration of my relationship with the people of Ruvu village. I tried to understand my neighbors, Saidi's extended family. After all, they're my family too, right? We may share similar DNA. However, despite being linked by a common religion, we were divided by centuries, cultures, language and education. I did not realize how huge the divide was at first. Eventually, I went on to do what so many other *mzungu*s do: work through the foundation from afar.

For me, the fourth incident was the straw that broke the camel's back. Eid-ul-Adha was approaching. Muslims who can afford to buy animals, typically a goat or sheep, slaughter them in remembrance of Prophet Ibrahim (Abraham) and his son's sacrifice and unwavering faith. The meat is then distributed with at least one-third going to the poor.

That year, I had received enough money in donations to buy 70 animals to be slaughtered and distributed among poor villages. Knowing that Ruvu had their own cows to slaughter during that time, I was reluctant to send an animal. But, with a last minute donation, we decided to send a sheep, my Walter.

In accordance with Islamic law, the animal cannot be slaughtered before the Eid prayer. If it is, it must be repeated. We arranged for the second and third *imam*s to pick the sheep up the day before Eid, so we were surprised when they showed up a day early. Accompanying them was Bint Masud's son; he calls me Auntie. It wasn't a problem though. Saidi gave them a basket to carry the sheep by bicycle, admonishing them for planning to pull the sheep three kilometers to Ruvu.

Unlike the previous year, we decided to pray Eid prayer in Ruvu. After the prayer, I asked, "Where is the sheep?" They told me it had already been eaten. I could not believe it. I tried my best to be pleasant because it was a holiday, but my outrage was clearly visible. You didn't need to speak English to know what I was thinking. How could they?

It was not the extra money or time that would be needed to find a replacement that upset me. It was the betrayal! The premature slaughtering of the sheep was done with impunity and full knowledge that it was in total violation of Islamic law. The next year, the foundation received enough donations for 18 cows, and 76 goats and sheep. The animals were distributed among 33 communities. My own village of Ruvu was absent from the list. Few asked why.

When I first moved to Jome, I thought I was bound to the people there by our professed faith. I've now realized that even our common religious bond had a crack that would take a new generation to repair. With a few exceptions, I turned away from our individual efforts to help Ruvu. My new focus was on building a foundation that would, hopefully, make systemic positive change.

CHAPTER 19

NO-LEGGED NEIGHBORS

One morning while Saidi was up doing chores, he heard the chickens crying. He went to see what was going on and saw a python with a dead, strangled chicken in his mouth. He quickly came in the house to get his steel rod weapon, which had been quite effective in the past. He threw the rod at the python, puncturing its side. Angered that he was being denied the meal he had just killed, the python lunged at Saidi with the rod still protruding from his back.

Unsuccessful, the python slithered off and hid in the rocks. Our nephew Musa showed up and suggested we try to burn it. "All I need is for him to show his head," Musa said. Then Musa's friend showed up. Everyone came with a new idea, and eventually they were able to kill him. I watched from a safe distance.

Sijoli, true to his name, reported that he had seen the python's tracks the week before. I hoped it was the same one. We measured the snake. It was an impressive 13 feet long. The poor chicken lay dead in the grass. Another chicken gone, another reason to build the brick compound wall.

About two years earlier, Saidi hired Mrs. Gazelle and her daughters to cut the grass behind the compound. He knew snakes would start to hide there if he let it get too long. With so many snakes around, I am often amazed that people are comfortable wearing nothing but plastic flip-flops—that is if they have shoes on at all. We made it a point to buy boots for everyone we hire. It is the least we can do. They seem appreciative.

As she cut the grass, I mentioned to Mrs. Gazelle that one of our hens who used to have four fairly large chicks now only had three. Shortly after, Mrs. Gazelle called out that she saw a python near where she was cutting.

Bakari, who was standing nearby, overheard our conversation. He was the only one wearing boots and would have been an ideal choice to go look for the snake, but he disappeared before we could ask for help. That's when the snake appeared, a constrictor.

Mr. Gazelle heard the commotion and came quickly, but before he could intervene, Mrs. Gazelle took her machete and smashed the snake. Mr. Gazelle got a few strikes in as well as their daughters looked on. At least the mystery of my missing chick was solved. Mrs. Gazelle and her daughters continued cutting the grass without a bit of trepidation.

Just weeks after the construction of the brick wall, Saidi showed me a picture of a snake Mrs. Gazelle saw outside the compound wall. It had raised up, puffed up its head and was ready to attack the chickens. It looked small in the picture, but the consensus was that it was a cobra. No one wanted to approach the snake. Their venom is very poisonous and can permanently blind you. After some discussion, Saidi decided to get some kerosene. He sprayed the area and the snake came out from the underbrush. It was disoriented. They finished it off with a wooden stick.

I found a dead chicken a few days earlier with no obvious wounds. Maybe this snake was the answer to that puzzle, but I think this relatively small snake's mother is still lurking around. I was growing accustomed to the fact, but not complacent, knowing we lived among some of the most lethal snakes on earth.

I added this incident into my mental list of why not to walk through tall grass and to scan the ground as I walk. As far as the chickens were concerned, our brick wall would help protect them in the near future. Any chicken that was foolish enough to fly over the wall does so at her own risk. The cocoon we created is not foolproof nor do we want it to be. With beauty, solitude and a little adventure comes risk.

After a little research, I concluded that the snake was a Mozambique spitting cobra. Their eggs are 10–22 in number. I pray the *kenge* (monitor lizard) helped itself. The following day, I saw a big land crab trying to penetrate the wall. No luck of course. I was grateful for the new brick wall. It helped with no-legged, four-legged and two-legged foes.

Another day, we noticed Mrs. Gazelle trying to get our attention from outside the compound wall. Saidi went out. "Don't you know where the bell is?" he asked. It was inside the grass *banda*. She said there was a snake lurking near the roof, right above the bell. Without any assistance, she killed the snake by smashing its head in. Women in the bush tend to be quite fearless.

I am guessing it was a black mamba. We had a very rainy February that year, so I think the poor snake was just looking for a dry place. I never want to kill an animal needlessly, but it is a matter of survival in the bush.

While I was in the kitchen one day, Saidi calmly said, "Do not come." You know what that means, right? I went. I found a chaotic scene. Saidi was running around, swinging his machete. The cat was running around, trying to catch the intruder. Trying to escape her two-legged and four-legged hunters, the long, bright green uninvited guest propelled itself from one side of the room to the other. Knowing she was trapped, the wingless, legless creature jumped around until she landed on the shoe rack. With one strike of the machete, she was gone.

Saidi threw the bloodied intruder out the front door. The chickens scrambled to come see, but they quickly moved on when they realized it was already dead. They went back to scratching and pecking for their usual meal: bugs.

Several layers of security are needed in the bush. Entry into our home requires opening a steel security door and a wooden door. The steel doors keep out two-legged predators. The wooden door keeps out the rest.

On his way out one day, Saidi opened the back wooden door. Like he had done countless mornings before, he reached for the locks of the steel doors. Thankfully, he looked up first. He saw a green mamba stretched out around the inner peripheral of the door. I heard Saidi's characteristic banging. I knew he was trying to kill an intruder. I thought, Could a rat finally have made it into my cocoon?

Saidi had trained me not to talk or yell out when he was on the hunt, so I quietly walked downstairs to find blood-stained tiles and our little Lindi looking at the aftermath. It did not take long for Saidi to think of a way to modify the steel doors to also keep out our no-legged neighbors. Two venomous green mambas in the house are two too many.

Our goats can sometimes be vocal, but one day I heard a sound I did not recognize. It was the sound of life being snuffed out. Living in the bush, which is full of strange sounds, you can get accustomed to ignoring things you hear and hoping they go away. That is exactly what we did, and it was probably our delay that led to there being two victims instead of one.

Eventually, Saidi said, "I must go." I reminded him not to forget his gun. I didn't want him out there unprepared. He went with Jiwe to the goat compound. I could see his flashlight from our bedroom window. Then I heard him say, "There is a path [python] in the goat *banda*. I am going to get Ali [our helper]."

He later told me that when he opened the *banda*, he could see the python curled around a pregnant goat in the nursery section where two moms, each with twins, were confined. Saidi knew from a previous encounter never to take on a python alone, so he and Jiwe went a half kilometer to where Ali and his family slept.

Rashid (our masonry *fundi*) and his helper were also sleeping there. I saw Rashid's motorcycle coming and then heard voices at the goat *banda*. Soon after, I heard three gun shots.

Saidi came to the house and asked me if I wanted to come see. When I walked cautiously into the *banda*, I saw two dead goats, a pregnant mom and her daughter. The head of the younger victim was covered in the saliva of the python. Apparently, the arrival of the entourage interrupted his early morning meal. We suspected that, after killing the mom, he found her too large to consume and opted for her daughter instead. I also saw the python, which was still alive despite being shot several times. The guys finished him off by repeatedly hitting his head.

We released all the goats from the scene of the crime. They all stayed away from the bodies except for the son of the deceased mom. He lay next to her body and grieved for his mother and twin sister. We buried the two bodies, hopefully deep enough to not attract a hyena. The remaining twin cried all night and through the next morning. I felt for him.

As I walk around and take in this beautiful land, I wonder if holes I see are the homes of rats, crabs or snakes. When passing under trees, I glance upward, knowing a snake may be eyeing me from above. People seem to have adjusted well to sharing the land with these feared no-legged neighbors, but it has taken me a bit of getting used to.

Snakes have been vilified from the beginning of time. Nevertheless, they are a crucial part of the balance of life. They, too, have their predators, but they have managed to survive through the ages. Our neighbors include cobras, pythons, green mambas and black mambas.

I recognize that they were here before me. I take solace in knowing that, most of the time, they stay to themselves. A sighting is rare, but they remind us every once in a while, "We are here. We have been here since the days of Adam, and we are not going anywhere."

CHAPTER 20

IT'S COMPLICATED

In Tanzania, your father's older brother is known as your big father, and his younger brother is your little father. Your mother's older sister is your big mother, and her younger sister is your little mother. Hence, all their children are your siblings. The children of Saidi's paternal siblings (from his big and small fathers) call him Father, but the children of his maternal siblings (from his big and small mothers) call him Uncle.

Initially, I was confused as to why Saidi had so many brothers and sisters. It took a while to understand the concept. Now I just ask who gave birth to whom and who was married to whom. I thought it was funny that a woman's grandson is considered her little husband, so Saidi always says my grandson Nuri is his biggest competition for my affection.

Usually, when I ask why I am addressed a certain way, Saidi says halfway through the explanation, "It is complicated." Most people have been married several times. Some have multiple wives as up to four are permissible in Islam, and few practice birth control. Just when I thought I had begun to understand and even respect the spaghetti connections that seem to roll off of people's tongue, Saidi said something new: "my sister from my slave mother."

Like most African Americans, the thought of slavery instantly conjures up images of whips and chains, scarred backs and calloused hands. I think of the largest known forced migration of peoples. There is no dispute that it was brutal. Slavery is inhumane. Nevertheless, I tried to put my preconceived notions aside so I could better understand.

I have read that the term "slavery" may be used to describe an institution that is oppressive but not as brutal as what my African ancestors endured in the Americas.

Years ago, the indigenous people of the land surrounding Jome had no currency. Services and goods were bartered. If the debtor had no other way of paying the debt, they would send a family member as payment. If you go to Ruvu today, elders can still point out the descendants of slaves. Yet, you cannot distinguish. It is difficult for me to understand how the unspoken label has not evaporated.

The first time I came to Ruvu, Saidi introduced me to a very old and wise woman named Bint Masud, which means "daughter of Masud." Saidi called her his sister. I asked how this could be, but he did not know. All he knew was that his father called her father "brother." As far as he is concerned, she is his sister and was a fixture in Jome when he was a child.

My curiosity and constant questioning finally led Saidi to ask one of his older brothers. As it turns out, Bint Masud is the granddaughter of someone who was the slave to Saidi's grandfather. Typically, the person who arrives as a slave eventually becomes a part of the new family, often marrying from the same family that so-called enslaved him or her. This is the case with Bint Masud.

Saidi's father's second wife is sometimes referred to by Saidi's siblings as their slave mother. She was given to Saidi's grandfather by her father to pay a debt. After toiling for a while, Saidi's grandfather suggested that she marry his son, Saidi's father. The offspring of the marriage between Saidi's father and his slave stepmother surround us today.

Saidi's father had 21 children, but only eight were from Saidi's mother, his last and only remaining wife when he passed away. Saidi has one living half-sister in a neighboring village from his slave mother, but he does not care to share much of the history from that side of his family. He remembers it was his half-sisters who came to Jome and stole his mother's jewelry and took his father's things after he died. He also remembers how much his mother, a young woman, cried.

Sometimes the family of the siblings from the other wives says all their family problems are from the slave side. Perhaps self-conscious about the rarely spoken label they bare, those from the slave side tend to behave in a more proud and arrogant way. I figure all families have their demons, and the feuds are not all related to these quiet designations.

There is a commonality among slavery of all kinds: people are stripped from their homeland and families. Usually, the new slaves were told by their own families that they were going for a visit somewhere. Then, they were just left.

Given the possible threat of a strapping young man around their wives, uncles would often ask their sisters to take their son (the uncle's nephew) as payment for a debt. The women were quite strong; they typically obliged. The uncles' fear was that, upon their deaths, the nephews would become suitors for their widowed wives, so the clueless victims would be sent off on a vaguely described trip, given food, housing and a new family name. Eventually, they would blend in with the family.

As an outsider, it is easy to be appalled by the concept. Yet, in the village today, all have the same opportunities—or lack thereof. There is no distinction by color, religion or family of origin. They are all equally poor, equally uneducated and equally vulnerable. I still do not fully understand it and probably never will.

Immersing myself in a different culture has taught me that I shouldn't judge something simply because it doesn't sit right with me personally. This understanding has made it easier for me to accept the term *mzungu*. For example, I realize most of Saidi's family calls me *mzungu* out of my earshot. I have begun to accept this. I even embrace it depending on the context.

I sometimes tease them if I see an improvement in their life. When we had to admit Mzee Ally into the hospital, we paid for an upgrade to what is called a "Grade 1" room. It is a single air conditioned room with its own bathroom. Unlike the typical toilets here and in much of the world, his toilet was not of the squat variety. Instead, he had a seated, western-style toilet.

Being elderly and nursing an injured ankle, he loved the toilet. I said to Mzee Ally, "You are now living like a *mzungu*." We decided to retrofit his home with a sit toilet.

When Saidi stops to talk to elderly people from the nearby villages, he will say, "Remember me? I am Kombania from Jome."

They often reply, "Kombania? Ah, you moved back with your *mzungu* wife." Seeing the sparkle in the eye of a *mzee* as they recall the old days of Jome is sometimes comforting. Their expressions tell me they are glad he is back and chose to return to his homeland with his *mzungu* wife.

I smile and then say, "*Shikamoo*."

They return a bigger toothless smile. "*Marhaba*." Then Saidi proceeds to tell me how this person is his uncle, grandfather, cousin or some other relative. If there is anything I have learned about living in the Motherland, it is that things are complicated and rarely as they appear.

A perfect example of this can be seen in our favorite guests, Luke and Sara. They are likely called *mzungu* because of their skin color. But despite their European ethnicity, they are truly African and know Africa much better than I do. Luke is Zimbabwean (born and raised, then kicked out by Mugabe), and Sara is British but grew up in South Africa.

I was slightly embarrassed by my naivety when they introduced me to their European looking friend. I asked twice where she was from, as if asking a second time would produce a different answer. Again, she answered that she was Kenyan. Finally, realizing I was still puzzled, she added that she was a third-generation Kenyan. I was so embarrassed. I mentally hit myself in the head. I had read enough dramatizations of the life of the early colonial Kenyans to know that Africa is complicated.

My pseudo European visitors seemed so comfortable in Jome, even more comfortable than this African transplant who spent her whole life longing to come back home. They hiked, swam and snorkeled. They all enjoyed bird and butterfly watching, but I was most amazed by their horticultural knowledge. This ex-New Yorker was the most timid in our group walkabout as I passed by the home of the 13-foot python we killed a few months earlier. I thought, so who is the real *mzungu?*

Even though titles and relationships can be difficult to define here, family is of the utmost importance. You can really see that in the way Saidi cares for his brother Mzee Ally, his oldest living sibling. Mzee Ally had been living in Dar with Rashid, one of their other brothers, but it wasn't working out. The problem was that Rashid wasn't actually living there. It was his second wife who was left with the responsibility of his care. Rashid spent most of his time on the island of Zanzibar with his first wife. Mzee Ally was in his 80's. He had poor eyesight, no income, no children and no wife, so we decided to bring him back to Jome.

Mzee Ally left Jome in 1952, before Saidi's birth. He left after being accused of stealing and selling the goat of his father's sister's son, who refused to pay Mzee Ally for some limestone he'd sold him. During the six-hour ride from Dar to Lindi, he taught me some of the family history that predates Saidi. He is quite the character.

Even though he hadn't been to the village since 1982, he could rattle off each village name as we passed by. According to Ally, Saidi's father died at the age of 114. He was pretty sure about that. Amazingly, he fathered children until his death. I have found no evidence to dispute this.

Without a proper house for Mzee Ally, he moved temporarily into our tent. Within a few months, he married someone from Ruvu. Unwilling to wait for the house we were building for him, his bride moved into the Jome tent. The marriage came as no surprise. We got suspicious when we noticed him looking spiffy, carrying fish, presumably, to his bride-to-be. He knew his bride from decades earlier, but being on the road all the time as a truck driver, nothing ever came of their relationship. Finally, they were together. True love. Well, not really. Their marriage lasted only a few months.

One year later, he was married again to someone else, perhaps for the 12th time. His memory was fading rapidly, and he got lost often. One day, we even had to send out a search party from several villages. We hopped in our car and hired motorcycles. Others headed out by foot. He was found the next morning, sitting under a tree. He said he may want to marry again, a younger woman so he can have children. He was thinking Mrs. Gazelle's sister-in-law. Saidi told him he was nuts, so he gave up on the idea.

On my 57th birthday, we decided to take a trip to Kayava, the birthplace of Saidi's father. That morning, Saidi asked, "Are you busy? What is your business today?" I am always amused by that question spoken from one retired person to another.

Saidi's father left Kayava after his father (Saidi's paternal grandfather) and his disabled brother (Saidi's paternal uncle) died. Saidi's father would make the journey almost on a daily basis to fish in Jome. Tired of making the trek, my father-in-law packed up what remained of the family and moved to Jome.

We grabbed our bottles of water and headed first to Ruvu to pick up Masudi, one of Saidi's other brothers. Masudi is the first born of Saidi's mother and father, or as they say here, "one mother, one father." Masudi had recently settled back in Ruvu from Dar. He knew the way to Kayava, so in the African way (no invitation, no planning), we went to see him. And in the African way, he said, "*Hakuna matata.*"

Within minutes, we were on our way. We stopped in the village of Kilolambwani to get directions. After some discussion with villagers about Kayava's inaccessibility by car, I popped my generic Claritin, grabbed my I-pod Shuffle and inhaler, and started walking with the group. After all, "It is not far!"

Finally, we made it to Kayava after a 45 minute walk. The heat of the day made it seem like much longer. I was glad I had worn my Keen hiking sandals. The trip was tough. Any other shoe would have been a bad choice. We found their grandfather's grave easily thanks to Masudi.

We visited the source of water for cows and saw the area where people say *jinn* (an unseen human-like being) live. The *jinn* that, presumably, have inhabited the area have been occasionally seen. They are described as *mzungus* of European descent. In other words, they are white. There are certain protocols for entering the area where the unseen live.

Masudi approached a large pool of water called Mgonya. It seemed like such an unlikely scene for a water starved area. The water is in a valley surrounded by rocky terrain. The stillness of the water, the absence of life, the glistening of the sun on its surface all made me think this could have been the first home of Adam and Eve.

Being a pragmatist, I dismissed those thoughts, then watched Masudi approach. He said, "*Hodi, Hodi, Hodi?*" before entering the area. *Hodi* is a Swahili word best translated as, "May I come in?" The response is usually, "*Karibu,*" meaning "welcome."

The legend of the not-so-distant past, maybe 20 years ago, is that a man with a cow entered that area and his cow just disappeared in the water. The cow's body was never found. He was warned not to go in that area with his cow, but he did not heed the warnings. Today, the designated cow drinking area is separate from where people and the *jinn* use water for their consumption. People believe if you do not ask permission to enter, you may see its residents, *mzungus*, swimming or sleeping on mattresses on top of the water.

Mgonya is where Saidi's extended family retrieved their water before moving to Jome. Allegedly, Saidi's father saw the *jinn* while living in Kayava. He fell sick shortly after. This may have sped up his exodus.

Saidi's brother Rashid also has a special connection to Kayava. It is the birthplace of Rashid and Mzee Ally. Taking advantage of the Dar-to-Ruvu buses, Rashid came for the annual Eid celebration in Ruvu and just stayed. Like his older sibling Mzee Ally, whom he cared for in Dar a few years earlier, Rashid left village life for the city as a young man. He left Jome with only the 3 schillings in his pocket, the equivalent of $0.001 US dollars today.

At the age of 77 and with no pension from his work as a retired construction worker, he decided to build a house in Ruvu and farm. He also built a *banda* in Kayava, his birthplace. Rashid told us, "I want to farm in Kayava and let people know we are back." In a vast country like Tanzania, even those with nothing in their pockets are not homeless. They have the land, and the land, despite being sometimes harsh, provides what is needed.

After Masudi, Saidi and I left Mgonya, we walked to a small river named Jalawa. I saw people collecting water in buckets. Women were doing laundry on its banks. We stopped and talked to several people. Saidi told some of the younger men to help an elderly man who had walked about 30 minutes to fill his bucket. He knew who we were, from Jome.

Young men had parked their bicycle on top of the ridge. After carrying the filled containers to their bicycles, they would return to their villages to sell the water to villagers who did not have the time or will. Depending on the time of year, Jalawa is the source of water for five villages, including Ruvu. Situated in a low area among the rocks, I enjoyed the brief reprieve from the day's heat.

After Jalawa, we headed back to the car. We passed Sijoli, who had brought the village cows for a drink. We were back to the car three hours after the start of our walkabout. Not far at all.

CHAPTER 21

IT IS JUST THE WAY IT IS

Receiving packages in rural Tanzania is a lesson in patience. I cannot predict bureaucracy, but I can look out for my best interest. My daughter sent me a small package that arrived at the Lindi post office. Because I asked the customs officer how he calculated the fees (25% of the value plus 18% VAT of the 25% value), he played by the rules.

In Lindi, there is no DHL office. The closest private courier service agent is in Mtwara, a two-hour drive south of Lindi. Nevertheless, they deliver to Lindi. The only challenge is clearing customs at the Dar airport. That is the part that truly requires patience.

I was thrilled to find that one of my favorite online clothing stores ships worldwide. I filled my online cart with two dresses, a pair of jeans and two tops. I used my Lindi P.O. Box address, hoping it would come via post office. But, like many other upscale suppliers, they shipped via DHL. I had much trepidation from a previous experience, and my fears were realized.

The package took only one day to reach Dar airport. I knew this because I signed up for alerts and had received a notification of "clearance processed," then "clearance delay." There was no more information after that.

Finally, I received a message about three days later requesting my personal tax identification number. I immediately complied and received a thank-you message by email. In the meantime, the agent in Mtwara was growing tired of me. She texted, "I will let you know when I have your package; there were no flights from Dar es Salaam to Mtwara." I was a veteran, so I knew not to rely on that information.

Determined to get some answers, I blasted all the Dar-based DHL contacts (about six) with an email. Finally, the customs supervisor forwarded my message to the inspectors who, within minutes, said they had finished inspecting my package. The next day, I received an "out for delivery" notification. Five days after arriving in Dar, the package was sent to Mtwara. It was Friday, and Monday was a holiday. The agent in Mtwara told me the amount due was 66,813 TZS ($40) for customs tax. She said I could pay the driver when he came to Lindi on Tuesday around 11:00 AM. I planned accordingly.

Eleven o'clock came and went. By 2:00 PM, I received a call from the courier that he did not know the location. We had agreed to meet at the LIFT office in Lindi town, but the courier now requested that we meet at the NBC Bank. Saidi and I rushed there but did not see a DHL truck. I called the number we had and saw a man outside the bank answer his mobile. We beeped the horn, and he came with a tattered parcel wrapped in clear plastic and tape that said, "Repackaged by DHL." I immediately became uneasy. Were my items OK? Were they all there?

Luckily, they were. I happily gave him 70,000 TZS ($42).

He rushed into the bank to make a photocopy of the paperwork I signed. Upon inspection of the multiple pages of customs and Tanzanian Revenue Authority paperwork, I noticed the declared value was only 139,000 TZS ($83). Effectively, the cost I paid to the Tanzanian government was 47% of the declared value. Vendors seemed to know that they would never have any customers if they did not "declare" something reasonable.

In addition to what seems a lopsided ratio for customs, I am often amazed at the cost of labor. It is the complete opposite of what I had experienced in the States, where you must pay close to $50 in labor charges just to have a problem looked at. Usually, for the cost of fuel and about $15, I can get a service call for most maintenance needs. That was a welcomed difference that took no getting used to.

But what I did have to get used to is all the counterfeit merchandise—and it is not even cheap sometimes. We have fake medicine, fake car parts, fake perfume, fake clothes and fake mobiles. There is a huge market for used clothes, books, office furniture and computers in Karikoo, Dar. They say you can have your leg stolen in the morning and buy it back in the afternoon. Of course, that's an exaggeration, but I get it.

Tanzania is rated as one of the most corrupt countries in the world. I am not sure how the watchdogs come up with these statistics, but I suspect part of the problem is the low salaries for government employees in powerful positions. To get your paperwork going, you often have to get past an employee whose job it is to move your file from one desk to the next. Because very few institutions have computerized their files, the power of the paper shuffler is magnified.

When I am frustrated, Saidi reminds me of the patience of a British expat who worked for an international NGO. His American wife wanted her car in Tanzania. A simple enough task, he thought. The car took 45 minutes to pass British customs and eight months to clear Kenya customs. Then, after the car sat in the port of Tanzania for six months, Saidi's boss asked him to do what he could. Unbeknownst to him (and all the other expats Saidi catered to), Saidi often used his own meager salary to get things moving. Fortunately, he was reimbursed by his grateful boss.

With few exceptions, processes that should take minutes take hours. Those that should take days take weeks, and those that should take months take years. There seems to be a tolerance for "good enough," but I resist the lull of such incompetency and corruption. After all, I have been taught some of the best project management practices, such as Six-Sigma, Lean Sigma, Zero-Defects, 7-Habits of Effective People and various others. The incompetency and unprofessionalism was enough to drive me nuts. These days, I still stick to my principals, but like any culturally sensitive expat, I have adapted.

Something else I adapted to is the theatrics of the televised parliament sessions. They are nothing like the slow, monotone sessions you find in America. Tanzanian parliament members know the problems and seem to know the solutions, but sometimes I think bureaucracy is by design, or maybe it is too difficult to move an elephant with a wheel barrow.

I am surprised at the patience of the Tanzanian people. They seem riveted by drawn-out parliament sessions, hoping that something positive will come from these often colorful exchanges between their representatives. Members of parliament bang tables with their open palms, expressing agreement or displeasure with their colleagues on the floor. Eventually, I grew to appreciate their methods. It is much better than the machete-waving bandits in the streets of our neighboring countries.

Like in any other country, Tanzanian politicians sometimes get caught up in scandals. One top government official was caught giving cell phones for votes. Another time, an ex-husband of a presidential candidate's wife claimed she had not divorced him before the candidate's marriage. His lawyer waved their marriage license on the local news, and the media showed wedding pictures, presumably of the distraught ex-husband.

I am somewhat skeptical that this woman would marry a high-profile politician without being divorced first. But as they say, power corrupts, but the pursuit of power is even uglier.

Here, it seems laws are enforced only sometimes, when it is most convenient. For example, Lindi City Council made a law that cows and goats couldn't roam the streets. It sounds reasonable and seems to work during business hours. However, every public holiday and late afternoon, the cows and goats return to the streets. City council members live in town. They know what is going on. I guess it is just a matter of priority.

As with other violations, citizens sometimes take matters into their own hands. Petty thieves are often relieved to see the police show up after they have been chased down by the entire neighborhood. The new victim knows the police will free him for a price. The unforgiving mob, on the other hand, will sometimes place him on fire. It is surprising that petty crime is still high with so much vigilante justice.

Because local thieves are not easily deterred, we had to take a step in building our home that I still haven't gotten used to: our otherwise postcard view is impeded by big metal security grills. Saidi has heeded my comments and offered to remove the upper floor seaside grills, but I changed my mind. Safety first. We aren't even located near a police station, and if the police were deployed, would they have enough fuel in their vehicles?

We were asked to contribute to the building of toilets so police can move into a building in Mchinga, 18 kilometers away. We pondered contributing building supplies but not cash. At least we would have a police force "nearby."

Sometimes I am pleasantly surprised by the community security forces at work. When a water drilling company tried to leave the area without drilling, the water-starved villagers blocked the road with large tree trunks in protest. I was impressed by the village's resolve but more impressed by the response. The police had to be deployed to open the road, which leads to six different villages, including Jome. The commander later told me they knew I, an American expat, was there.

I am happy to see that LIFT isn't the only organization working to improve the situation of people in Tanzania. According to the UN-GA (UN Global Assembly), countries like Tanzania have fallen short in their goals of reducing maternal mortality and eradicating poverty.

Malaria is still the biggest killer in Tanzania. One of the most effective ways to combat it is the use of treated mosquito nets, but villagers tend to have other plans for their nets. They use them as barriers for their crops to keep out goats and chickens. This was reported on the news, but I've seen it with my own eyes. Additionally, the funding from international donors for the insecticide that treats the mosquito nets was not renewed.

When the officials brought mosquito nets for distribution in Ruvu, I asked the Ruvu village chairperson if they were being used as fishing nets. "Oh, yes," he said. "There are not many mosquitoes in Ruvu." He was right. Between the ocean breeze and the long dry season, mosquitoes are harder to find in Jome and Ruvu.

We have other menacing biting insects, but I blame my annual bouts of malaria on my occasional overnight visits in Dar or Lindi town. Ever since the government banned small-mesh fishing nets because they are ecologically unfriendly, the people began to use mosquito nets in their place. They have asked the government many times to offer fishing nets with larger mesh, but their request has not been met.

Knowing that few people have access to banks or any type of business financing, Saidi and I thought it a good idea to try to get a Village Savings and Loan (VSL) branch in our area. We first had to verify that the model was *halal*, that is, free of illegal interest.

We met with people from the Aga Khan Foundation to discuss the details. They told us of a project to start 4,500 VSLs in the Lindi and Mtwara regions. Saidi and I made an informal agreement with them to help in Ruvu and the other villages surrounding Mchinga. No matter how disenchanted I become with the people of Ruvu, I can never give up on them. They are my family. I cannot break our bond.

A few months earlier, we passed a group of adult women from Ruvu on the road. We stopped to take their picture as they were dressed nicely and seemed jovial from their trip to Mchinga for a *Dhikri* ritual. Saidi asked how many of them had completed primary school. The answer was none, a sad and common fact. In my newness to the area, I still thought I could move mountains.

Saidi told the women some of the ideas I was working on. It was these women who originally inspired our inquiry into getting VSL groups in the area. I was also inspired to help these women and others like them learn more about health and sanitation issues. I was naive enough to think I could get help from government officials to train a Ruvu woman as a village health worker. Silly me.

I had been following two leads. The Aga Khan lead was working out for the VSL idea. For health education, I was referred by an acquaintance to the Lindi regional health secretary. He referred me to the region's social protection officer, who then referred me to someone else, who then referred me back to the village government.

Discouraged, I gave up on a government intervention. They know the problem and, for one reason or another, do not have the capacity to help. I concluded the answer was in the private sector, maybe even my own foundation, which was still only a twinkle in our eye at that point.

Despite the challenges, of all the countries in Africa, I am thankful I landed here in the home of the Serengeti and Kilimanjaro. Tanzania has a history of religious, ethnic, tribal and political coexistence and tranquility. Dar es Salaam translates to "House of Peace." That's exactly what it is for the most part. For example, the foreign minister, who is Christian, has built mosques in Muslim villages. Since its independence and not by referendum or constitution, the presidency has alternated between Christians and Muslims. Politics here are not without problems, but they are superior to those of our continental neighbors. Tanzania has been a place of retreat for countless refugees from Rwanda, the Republic of Congo and Burundi. And of course, I have found a new home here as well.

CHAPTER 22

EDUCATION

It is no accident that the foundation made education the center of its framework. It is a lack of education that causes much of the economic disparities. However, it is difficult to convince people that they need school when they struggle to fill their bellies daily. Convincing parents and children that going to school will change their lives is no easy task, and I see why when I look at the condition of government schools. If the schools created by the government, the most powerful body in the land, are scarcely maintained, what message does that send to the people?

The approach to education in Tanzania truly shocked me. Ruvu Primary School has no potable water and no power. The classrooms are dreary, and the walls and floors are crumbling. Teaching aids are nonexistent. For several years, we have complied with teachers' requests to help with the cost of typing and photocopying exams. We have received many letters from teachers requesting red marking pens, atlases, chalk, even cement to fix the buildings.

Once a teacher sent us a letter that itemized the cost for complete modifications to a school building that was earmarked to house

Ruvu's teachers. We had to become more selective with our assistance. We had already been providing the ingredients for the soon-to-end daily porridge program.

It is hard to have high expectations of students when the schools do not meet their needs. Money doesn't guarantee a quality education, but it makes it much more attainable. The year we received a donation of enough English textbooks for the entire school, Ruvu had an unprecedented 18 students to pass Standard 7. One of those students was sponsored by a friend to attend the private secondary school in Lindi. And Hasan, who was now mobile with his new wheelchair, enrolled the following year as a first-year student at the age of 12. Three years later, all eight of Ruvu's Standard 7 children failed. No one seemed surprised. No one seemed to care.

The problem is the way the students are taught and the education levels of the teachers. They are expected to prepare students for their capstone national exam given in their last year of primary school. To succeed in the subsequent years, English is required. English is the official national business language. Yet, Saidi must often translate to the teachers and headmaster when I strike up a conversation with even the most educated the area has to offer. National exams at the secondary level are in English, but most students who tell me they completed secondary school can barely give Basic English greetings. No wonder the children struggle to pass exams. The teachers do not even know the subjects they teach.

There is no surprise the failure rate is high. Each year, it is expected that significantly more students will fail than pass. Instead of nurturing creativity and teaching problem solving skills, the system seems to encourage "teaching to the test." Students study only the specific information they need to know to pass. They never gain a comprehensive understanding of the material. And these partially educated students go on to become teachers.

It is no wonder administrators and politicians are now crying that they do not have enough math and science teachers. The strategy does not work. Because Tanzanians receive a substandard education, their job possibilities are few. They are usually left to choose from a pool of menial jobs. The road engineering, gas exploration, mining and all other lucrative jobs are contracted out to Europeans and Asians. Those who do manage to pass their exams are usually happy with low-wage government jobs. They supplement their salaries with whatever perks they can squeeze out of the system.

The Tanzanian education system sounds like it would produce highly educated students. It offers 13 years of schooling, 11 of which are mandatory. Students are required to complete seven years of primary school (Standard 1 through Standard 7), then four years of secondary school (Form 1 through Form 4). A few make it to two years of high school (Form 5 and Form 6). Those who fail have no choice but to spend money (if they have it) to go to the array of marginally better private schools.

Going to private school is out of the question for the poorest village children, but parents who have the means and desire often do not wait for failing grades. They ship their young children to private boarding schools as soon as they can. In Lindi town, most of the middle class parents are empty nesters as their children, even the young ones, have already been shipped to Dar to live with a relative while they go to school.

Ironically, students who fail secondary school automatically qualify for a number of private so-called colleges. Those who have the money attend these private institutions and are then circled back into the system to return as primary school teachers. The cycle of incompetence continues. When our great niece failed secondary school for the second time, she told us she qualified for an education college. Saidi replied, "So you want to teach how to fail?"

It is a dangerous state of affairs having so many jobless, unskilled, uneducated young people, but there is one bright spot: the government technical schools. They offer short and long courses in several disciplines, including computing, driving, hotel management and auto repair. However, as is typically the situation here, the cost is beyond the reach of those in rural communities.

In order to bring real opportunities to the people of rural Tanzania, everyone must have access to free education through high school. It is not truly free if the students must pay for uniforms, housing and even their own desks, which is currently the requirement for "free" secondary school education.

Aside from the flawed setup of the school system, another problem is the huge number of unsupervised students living on their own. There simply are not enough students who pass primary to warrant the building of secondary schools close to each village. As a result, the ones who pass and have parents willing to support their higher education are dislodged from their homes at the tender age of 13 or 14. Without adequate dormitories, the parents who do not have relatives in the area are required to rent rooms for their children.

Only the most disciplined and mature teen can overcome the social temptations of unsupervised freedom at this most vulnerable age. One year, a Tanzanian who married a *mzungu* decided to pay all school fees and buy uniforms for all the children who passed primary. That first year of secondary, 50% of the girls were pregnant. No wonder parents who can afford it opt for pricier boarding schools. The poorer, more socially conservative parents just keep their children home, especially the girls.

Though I am a public school advocate, I understand why so many strive to send their children to private boarding schools. It is not about the pomp and circumstance of having a child in private school (as is sometimes the case in the States). It is a matter of survival. Their only hope for a decent job making a livable wage is to get the best education possible. The parents who realize this do all they can to protect their children's chances at a better life.

Given the importance of boarding schools, I was excited when I was offered the opportunity to volunteer as an English teacher at a private boarding secondary school. On my second day, their regular

English teacher did not show up. The school figured the students and I could communicate effectively.

I was glad I knew from previous encounters which American words to avoid. Here, a store is called a shop or market; an elevator is called a lift; and soccer is called football. We all learned together as English grammar is definitely not my strength. I stuck to the English books I brought from the States. They were a lifesaver.

It is funny to see the random things the students know about America. They did not know what a cruise or skiing was, but they knew Arnold had been the governor of California. The power of TV, I guess. I asked the students what they wanted to do after school. This is what I recollect: 1 pilot, 1 football player (i.e., soccer), 1 politician, a couple of journalists, a women's doctor (i.e., Ob/Gyn), a lawyer, a soldier, a shop keeper, a few accountants and many teachers. I only hope they are supported and pushed hard enough to make these dreams a reality.

By the second weekend of class, I had become worried that the girls seemed too passive. I attempted to draw everyone in by talking slowly and requesting feedback, but the girls weren't speaking up. I didn't want them to think it wasn't their place to have thoughts and opinions. I tried my best to awaken something in them, but it didn't seem to work.

As a *mzungu* teacher at a Tanzanian school, I had to get on my soap box about being on time. I couldn't understand why, knowing their cultural tendencies, the school administration picked 8:00 AM on Saturdays and Sundays for the class. Saidi and I often missed breakfast to assure I was on time.

My patience had grown short. I felt I had something to offer but wanted to teach students who actually wanted to be there. I was teaching a Form 4 class, the last year of secondary education in a private boarding school. These students were privileged to be in a position most others never get access to, but they wouldn't even come to class on time. If they did not want to be there, neither did I.

Not wanting to be a quitter, I stuck it out a few more weeks, but the breaking point was when I arrived one day and no one was there. Finally, the liveliest and brightest students came and informed me that they were expecting visitors from another boarding school and had been busy cleaning the premises. The students were polite and apologetic, and they seemed surprised that no one had informed me. Like so many cases before, I left. No one called. It just ended. I wondered if my failed experience as a volunteer teacher was a reflection of my teaching ability or the entrenched custom of paying someone to learn.

Daddy taught me that it was a privilege to learn from someone that had something to offer. Grab it wherever and whenever you can get it. I was accustomed to paying out my own pocket, or in some cases asking my employer to pay, for the privilege of keeping my skills sharp. You can imagine that I was surprised by the prevailing practice of paying someone to learn. A Tanzanian student of a continuing education class often expects to be paid a daily allowance to attend. No allowance, and the teacher will likely find a sparsely populated classroom, even if the class is free. If this is the practice of continuing adult education, I concluded that I should not have been surprised that less than 30% of students in my region enrolled in the first year of secondary school reach the last and fourth year. Of those that reach the last year of secondary school, only 20% pass the national exam and advance to high school. [2]. I believe self-improvement requires attaining new skills. It takes time and sometimes money. No pain, no gain!

---

[2] Source: Basic Education Statistics Tanzania 2012.

CHAPTER 23

LIVING OFF THE SEA

Jome was empty when I first arrived. Other than a few fishermen who would camp out on the beach, no one was to be found. I had assumed there would be no need for the notorious brick wall other houses had. Clearly, I was wrong. It must have been our reopening Jome that attracted all the new life.

I had visited Pacific and Atlantic beaches in the US. I had even experienced the undertow and the tide. But until I arrived in Tanzania, I had not seen such dramatic changes in the coast. "Where does all the water go?" Saidi asked me once. I had to Google it.

I was reminded of my high school science lessons about our dependency on the gravitational forces among the sun, moon and our planet. The answer still baffles me when I try to imagine everything shifting as we spin, circle and pass by other extraterrestrial matter. We are in constant motion and cannot feel it. But one thing is for sure: if things stop moving, we are doomed. Partly out of laziness and partly because my understanding felt incomplete, I just told Saidi, "The moon pulls it to a different area." I was happy he seemed satisfied and did not probe more.

Though the dramatic changes in the shore are discouraging for beach-loving swimmers, they provide a livelihood for so many. Sea farmers, primarily women, converge in Jome at low tide to manage their *mwani* farms. *Mwani* is a kind of seaweed that serves as a cash crop for the locals. When the tide is low, *Mwani* farmers rush out to pick their crops.

The tree branches that the farmers affix to the ocean floor protrude from the ocean floor, letting everyone know the tide has yet to return. The branches are used to secure the ropes. Each farmer starts with a small seedling that grows like a vine on the ropes. After harvest, they dry it on the beach. It is sold for about $0.35 per kg. Nothing to get rich off of, but it allows many villagers to feed their families. The more successful farmers hire *pikepike* drivers to pick up their large yields. In a place rife with poverty, *mwani* is a critical component of the local economy. Many women who joined the VSL contributed from their *mwani* income.

Mzee Ally does not have a farm, but he can be seen each morning collecting what loose *mwani* he can find. We worry sometimes about his safety, out there in the ocean without adequate vision, but at least he's getting good exercise. I guess he can't help that he prefers the harvest of the sea over that of the land.

The farmers use makeshift flags to identify their spaces, but thieves are not deterred. We have heard the occasional screams of women who discovered their harvests had been stolen. I heard a farmer frantically ask Mzee Ally once, "Have you seen my *mwani?*"

"Do I look like the *mwani* police?" he snapped.

There is never a dull moment with Mzee Ally. He keeps us on our toes and reminds me of the beloved elders I left behind back in the States.

I will never forget the time he ventured off on what was supposed to be a quick trip to buy rice. The entire day went by and he hadn't returned. It was high tide, so everyone advised him not to take the ocean road, but Ally can be stubborn. Hours later, a fisherman found him, rice in hand but naked from the waist down. The rushing water had washed away his *shukr* (a wrapped garment worn by Muslim men).

The fisherman put Mzee Ally in a *banda* and meant to inform his family, but he forgot, probably because of his bangi indulgence. Forgotten, our poor Mzee Ally stayed in that *banda* all night until word got to our nephew in another village that his uncle was naked and waiting to be escorted home. Saidi, our nephew and one of the helpers made the trek through the night to the *banda*. When they got close, they called out to Mzee Ally. "I am here!" he responded, happy to hear familiar voices.

"Do you have the rice?" they asked him playfully.

"Yes, but my *shukr* is gone," he called back. We still laugh about that story to this day.

One month prior to my first trip to Tanzania, we celebrated my daughter's marriage. She selected a sea theme, so I bought sea shells on the internet. She placed them in curved glasses of sand, each glass tied with ribbon. It was quite picturesque and creative on her part. Everyone loves the (albeit fake) beauty of the sea. Little did I know that a mere year later, I would construct a house directly on the beach, surrounded by a breathtaking view of the ocean and more shells than I knew what to do with.

I often see children combing the beach for shells to sell. They receive about $0.50 per kg. As I began to calculate the children's insignificant take-home pay, I felt guilty. To the end user, these shells are mere decoration— for a living room, a reception hall, a necklace or maybe an ethnic hairstyle. To the hardworking children who collect them, they are a way to get enough money for dinner.

It is amazing how the farmers know when the water will come and go. Most of them live inland, but they arrive right before the water recedes and return home just as the coast fills in again. This ocean, which is so mysterious to me, seems to have been demystified by those who rely on its gifts.

The fishermen seem to have mastered its rhythm. They navigate dhows with little more than a homemade sail. Most fishermen rely on the tide to pick out what fish they can capture from the shallow water. Even though it is their living, they are patient and trusting of the sea. There is a powerful lesson in it all.

A moonless night is the best time for many fishermen. Using kerosene lamps, they can see the fish. As the tide comes in, Saidi often searches for returning fishermen, hoping he can buy the day's dinner. Of course, the best fish comes from those with the means to go into the deeper waters, but we aren't picky. I'm just happy to eat fresh meat that was still alive just hours earlier. That isn't the norm where I come from.

Our first few years in Jome, the voice of the ocean was often disrupted by explosions. Fishermen frequently used the banned practice of bombing and capturing. They did not care that they were killing the coral, fish eggs and smaller fish. They only cared that it was a quick and effective way to get a lot of fish. But then we would hear complaints that fishing was not as good as it used to be. Hmm, I wonder why.

Occasionally, we'd hear of fishermen losing their fingers and even lives because of the bombs. We heard of one unfortunate soul whose body was dragged to land and abandoned in the bush by his fishermen friends, too afraid of being caught—but still, they bombed.

Injured fishermen would go to underground doctors as the practice had a severe punishment. Eventually, the government cracked down. Our previous village chairman had received compensation from the unscrupulous fishermen to keep quiet, but the current chairman is facing jail time if there is any more bombing. He is much stricter on enforcement. A natural resource officer is stationed in Mchinga but only makes occasional patrols. For a time, the bombing stopped. The fish are much more plentiful now.

The sad thing about living in the bush is that the repercussions from the fishermen seem worse than those from the authorities. The bombing resumed. I wanted to report it, but Saidi doesn't want to risk our house being bombed. He tells me to keep quiet. Others keep quiet, too.

As powerful as the fishing bombs are, they pale in comparison to the power of the ocean. Sometimes, the ocean seems satisfied. Other times, it becomes thirsty. It yearns for more water. That's when it rains.

We received a call one day from our guard, Ali, while in town. He said, "Mvua nyingi sana." Translation: "There is heavy rain." I've learned that when a native says rain is coming, believe it. The rain came down in torrents as we drove home. We successfully passed known troubled areas, including a bridge built by the Germans about a century ago. We also passed our neighbor's house and farm. It was completely flooded, more water than I had ever seen. Everyone growing the local sesame cash crop was devastated.

We had a relatively smooth trip almost all the way, right up until we reached the stone bridge leading to our home. The approach to the bridge is downhill, and then you must go uphill. It is nearly impossible to make it without four-wheel-drive. It is a potentially hazardous area we constantly pamper to make sure the delivery trucks can get through.

That day, there was no getting through with all that rushing water. Briefly discussing the possibility of sleeping in the car, we waited an hour and a half for the conditions to improve. While we waited, Saidi told me to unbuckle my seatbelt in case our car got swept away. He told me the secret of the river is never to cross when it is a foot or more high. It was definitely higher than a foot.

After a small break, the rains returned later that night. The color of the ocean changed, indicating the mixing of rain water with salt water. The ocean had quenched its thirst, for now.

It seems the villagers along the sea think the ocean yearns for more than just water. Apparently, they think it wants whatever they do not want. Once I complained to an elder about the plastic bottles that wash up on our beach. His response was that "this younger generation of women does not take the garbage far out like their predecessors." I couldn't be that surprised; this was the same *mzee* who thought nothing of a verified rapist moving back into the home with the stepdaughter he raped.

As important as the ocean is, it is even more important for a water-starved area. Its water is useful for washing pots and even flushing pit hole toilets. The problem is that many in the villages do not have toilets but instead view the ocean as one big toilet bowl.

Building toilets is one of the foundation's goals, but education is first. Until people understand why they need toilets, they won't make it a priority. Even if given the means, most people will invest in aesthetic changes to their homes before building a toilet. I've seen it happen. Only one person in Ruvu took us up on our offer to buy porcelain squat toilets if they dug and prepared the septic hole. I am thankful Ruvu is only a small village. I am sure the ocean is even more thankful.

CHAPTER 24

BON APPETIT

Dinner invitations were plenty during my visits to Libya, and the variety of dishes was bountiful. My ex-in-laws constantly presented various savory delights in front of me. If I was full, they got disappointed and thought it was an indication of my distaste for their food. In this regard, my Libyan family is not unique as I have found Arab hospitality to be the best and the food fantastic.

In my 24 years married to a Libyan-American, I found it hard to compete with my in-laws and friends. I tried to learn as ternal m

much as I could, but there was so much and I could never quite do enough. Those days were full of invitations, pot-lucks and enjoyable gatherings. On my second day in Tanzania, my host organization's country director invited me to lunch at a Lebanese restaurant. It was familiar and delicious, but it was as close as I got to a Libyan experience.

But even without all the dinner invitations, Tanzania still has delectable food. One of my favorite things is that like in Libya, I can eat most of the meat dishes. With a substantial Muslim population, most restaurants have *halal* (like the Muslim version of Kosher) menus.

Of course, the discriminating palate still has to be wary. During my first visit to the town of Masasi, Saidi took me to the market to show me *samaki mchanga*, meaning "sand fish," a misleading name for a rat! The Christians belonging to the Makua and Makonde tribes eat it. They say the Wakutu in Morogoro eat it as well. I can't verify any of that. All I know is that I do not eat it.

As we walked the market, I braced myself to see dead rats hanging in front of vendors' food stands. Fortunately for me, they were all sold or in short supply. I decided from that time on that if there was meat on the menu, I would definitely ask what kind.

The simplicity of Tanzanian food puts me at ease. It is not intimidating despite its many East Indian influences. Spices such as masala and tandoori are regularly found in the markets, and Zanzibar is famous for its clove farms. In fact, tea is often mixed with a masala spice. But for the average Tanzanian, the menu may include bananas in coconut milk, fried or dried fish (complete with head and tail), rice or *ugali*, fresh red beans and a green vegetable.

Ugali is a staple food, a necessity in the village. It is made from *unga* (flour) that has been mixed with water and cooked with constant stirring to make a dough-like mix. The white, tasteless end product is plopped on the plate with some kind of accompanying sauce.

Though it is common for Muslims to use the Islamic tradition of eating most dishes with their hands, even Christians eat *ugali* without utensils. The dough is grasped in the hand and dipped into its companion dish. *Mzungu* restaurants avoid serving *ugali*, but it is a must in local restaurants that cater to indigenous Tanzanians.

Forks and spoons are rare in local restaurants, so it is common for waiters or waitresses to not even think to offer them. However, if you ask, they will gladly provide them. All local restaurants have a sink in the eating area for patrons to wash their hands before and after the meal. Napkins are less common.

I have never been one to enjoy cooking, but I love for people to enjoy my food. Thanks to the simplicity of the food here, I can get away with preparing a dish of rice pilau; green vegetables; and fish, chicken or goat masala. I am also relieved that Saidi is not picky. When we do not have guests, we dine on rice and green leafy vegetables most days. If Saidi wants *ugali*, he buys it at a local restaurant. If he wants something with bananas, he buys that as well. (I'm not a banana fan.)

On any given day, I keep the pantry stocked with basmati rice, various pastas and fresh red beans. I keep fresh vegetables in the refrigerator, but it doesn't always work. Without reliable refrigeration, the menu is usually decided based on whichever vegetable is about to go bad first. On the rare occasion that we decide we need protein other than beans, we kill one of our chickens or buy freshly caught fish. Goats are reserved for guests, and the quantity of meat left over means our neighbors and family in surrounding villages will also get meat. Remember, nothing goes to waste in Africa.

We eat rice or pasta daily. Rice is grown locally and sold in bulk. The price per kilogram depends on the quality. I learned that there are three different names for rice. Before milling, it is *mpunga*. After milling and before cooking, it is *mchele*. Cooked rice is called *wali*. To avoid the lengthy pre-cooking cleaning ritual, I prefer the imported basmati rice at three times the price. In true *mzungu* fashion, I will gladly pay for convenience.

For breakfast, we typically eat a Spanish omelet with bread. Even though we have a large number of chickens, I buy eggs in the market. I do not have the discipline to visit the chicken house every day. Being anal about food, I do not trust the chain of custody of eggs from my own chicken house to my kitchen unless it is Saidi or me. Not knowing which eggs are fresh and which have been abandoned long ago, I play it safe and buy them at the market.

Occasionally when assured the eggs are freshly laid, I have supplemented my market-bought eggs with Jome eggs. On the rare occasion that I prematurely run out of eggs, Saidi will go to the chicken house only to return empty handed, saying all the hens are sitting. During my days of volunteering at a Michigan food pantry, I learned that eggs can last weeks unrefrigerated if they have never been washed or previously refrigerated. So, like most places in the world, my tray of eggs sits on a shelf with only an occasional rotten one found.

My Spanish omelets, yummy as they are, are no competition for my morning coffee. It is true that East Africa really does have the best coffee, and it is cheap. Instead of paying $5 for the likes of Starbucks or Biggby Coffee, I drink a cup of strong Tanzanian coffee for the equivalent of $0.05.

Saidi and I couldn't share our lives together without sharing our cultural foods. I introduced him to peanut butter sandwiches, hummus and couscous (albeit some I had embraced from my past). He enjoyed them all. He introduced me to *ugali*, sugarcane juice, coconut milk and cassava. My first exposure to cassava was in the form of chips that were sold on Coco Beach in Dar. They are eaten more frequently in the villages though. There, it is peeled and boiled or even eaten raw.

Cassava is a root that is about 75% carbohydrates. I had a very negative opinion of it when I first came to Tanzania. I read it was not native to Africa and was introduced by invaders. Its introduction into the African diet replaced more nutritional, native foods. My opinion eventually softened when I saw it can save populations from hunger because it can be grown in a sometimes harsh climate. Now when I need a little breakfast variety, I add cassava to the menu. Additionally, its green leafy vegetables provide much-needed vitamins to our diet.

In the States, people drink coconut milk in a pouch or can. Here, you drink it straight from the fruit. The meat is grated and squeezed, forming a juice that is used in rice, cassava and banana dishes. I have tried grating fresh coconut myself but prefer the readymade packages. Sugarcane juice is available in Zanzibar and Dar. It is a tourist delight.

Another tourist delight is seeing all the pretty displays of seasonal fruit. The markets and streets are full of merchants and middlemen trying to sell mangoes, oranges, melons and pineapples during the harvest season. I notice I feel healthier when the time from the farm to my stomach is days, not weeks. I believe that's how it should be.

CHAPTER 25

BEATING THE ODDS

As we embrace our second chance at love, we both know there is a big elephant in the room: our health. What one person lacks is compensated by the other, so it is difficult for us to imagine life without each other. Still, we can't deny the inevitable. It is unlikely, but only God knows if we will be like the couple in the renowned lovers' grave in Bagamoyo, Tanzania. As the story goes, a husband and wife drowned and were found holding each other. Of course, we do not want to drown, but it would be lovely to go together, wrapped in each other's loving arms.

Saidi hates talking about it, but I sometimes force the issue to minimize the impact of what will surely come. It took some arm twisting, but I convinced him to let me buy our burial shrouds. I do not trust that those in the village could assist. Muslims are not embalmed, and burial should be as soon after death as feasible. I didn't want to wait until it was too late.

My Muslim sisters in Kalamazoo, Michigan, taught me how to wash and wrap a deceased woman's body to prepare for burial. I bought the material and followed the instructions to cut one set for a man and one for a woman. They are stored away in our closet, out of sight but never out of mind.

The only complication is that, as an American *mzungu*, Saidi would need some kind of death certificate to report my passing. I still do not know how that will be resolved, but it is not a major concern.

In addition to completing what little we could in advance to help a distraught partner, we take any signs of potential health problems seriously. Saidi and I attempt to institute a lifestyle that will, God willing, keep us healthy.

But of course, no one can avoid sickness forever. Even with all my treated mosquito nets, I finally caught malaria. It felt like the flu. I mean a bad case of the flu: alternating chills and sweats, headache, dizziness, loss of appetite, and body weakness. I was on anti-malaria medicine for my first few trips to Tanzania, but that is not sustainable beyond the first three years of permanent relocation. Taking the meds past that can lead to liver damage.

With the malaria came shortness of breath. I self-diagnosed pulmonary edema and helped things along with a diuretic. I wanted to take Malarone for the malaria as it is the anti-malarial prescribed in the States that I was familiar with, but it was not known by any of the "health professionals" in Lindi. Before giving up, I contacted a pharmacist in Dar who caters to expats. I was relieved to find that he stocked it, no prescription needed. Maybe next time I thought.

The first medicine I was given made me feel better for a short while, but my malaria must have been strong. The sickness came back. I was then given quinine sulfate. Between the side effects from the treatment and the symptoms from the malaria, I couldn't eat or drink a thing. Dehydrated, I was given IVs at home and I stopped the quinine. Big mistake. Things got worse.

Saidi took me to St. Benedict's Ndanda Hospital, about an hour and a half southwest of Lindi. They advised me to get back on the quinine, but this time I forced myself to eat. Saidi does not cook, but he tried. He called his rice "food for life." In other words, forget the taste. I finished the quinine sulfate but had shortness of breath. Little by little, I regained my strength and my breathing improved. My last quinine dose was a celebration, taken one day before fasting for the beginning of *Ramadan*.

Now that I had actually experienced malaria, I became even more vigilant about using treated mosquito nets. They are one of the best ways to prevent it, but the USAID grant to supply the insecticide has dried up. I got that insider tip from a visiting fellow.

After I wash our mosquito net, Saidi soaks it in the toxic brew. We can no longer find the treatment in Lindi, but we found a pharmacy with a small supply in Mtwara. We happily cleaned them out of their inventory. Now I just had to remember to put down the nets before dusk, a task that sounds much easier than it really is.

St. Benedict's Ndanda Hospital gave me more reassurance than the government hospitals I have visited. The nurses wore crisp white uniforms; there was soap at the sinks; and the beds had clean sheets. You could see the sisters (nuns) around the compound. It was comforting to see a hospital that actually looked like it could help when in need.

On my second trip to Ndanda, I was having pain in my eye. Not wanting to wait in a long queue, Saidi told them we wanted Grade 1 care. He told me to speak only English, as if I was fluent enough to speak Swahili. The guard told us it would be expensive, but he escorted us to a nursing station in the rear of the compound nonetheless.

A nurse completed my registration card and then escorted us to the optometrist. I was taken immediately, ahead of those waiting. The optometrist completed a card documenting my symptoms and recorded the results of the vision test.

I was then escorted to the doctor's office. It was locked. Maybe he was at lunch, I thought. We waited with others for about 45 minutes. The diagnosis: dry eye. The treatment: artificial tears. When it was all done, I had to pay for the registration card and office visit. The cost for the Grade 1 exam and registration: 5,000 TZS or $3.50. I spent

4,000 TZS or $2.80 at the hospital's pharmacy for the artificial tears. I was told that if I come back again (e.g., malaria), I should go to the rear building since I am now registered as a Grade 1 patient. The worlds of capitalism and socialism meet.

I began to adjust to managing my health in Tanzania. Thankfully, the generic equivalents of my necessary prescription drugs are available over the counter. I usually verify the dosing regimen on the internet. My biggest fear is to be an inpatient in a hospital reminiscent of the 1960s, complete with shared, outhouse-style bathrooms. I do have to use laboratory services in Lindi at times for things like malaria, but even that is a shot in the dark.

The bathrooms at both government and private hospitals and clinics used by patients to give a urine sample make you forget you are in a health facility. Imagine giving a urine sample in a bathroom with no lights, no soap and no running water.

One time, the regional hospital mixed my malaria results with Mzee Ally's. I discovered it when I kept waiting for my results and noticed he was done. He had talked to the physician, who I guess did not notice he was not a 56-year-old woman. Thankfully, both of us tested negative. Not wanting to wait in a long queue just to be told I was negative, we just left.

When we first moved to Lindi, Saidi tried to reassure me that there was a high quality clinic in the region, owned by German expats. On my first visit, I was asked if I wanted VIP or regular registration. VIP is $7, twice the price of regular registration. The VIP treatment allows you to skip the line and go straight to the doctor, who is really not a doctor. However, you still have to wait in queue for the lab technician.

While waiting, a patient before me threw her blood-stained cotton ball in the same container with the clean, alcohol-soaked ones being used for new patients. Everyone groaned. The technician threw the soiled cotton ball in the waste container but continued to use the other now-suspect cotton balls. I resisted the urge to protest. I just wanted to fit-in with the others.

As we waited to be seen, my fellow patients and I continued to slide down the bench. Finally, it was my turn. When I took my container to the bathroom to give a urine sample, I discovered there was no soap or water. I was shocked that a clinic that locals held in such high regard had such poor sanitation standards. How does a hospital not have soap and water? Yet, locals wait in queue to visit because it is owned by *mzungus*.

Saidi and I had been planning to register at Aga Khan Hospital in Dar. Finally, during one of our business trips to Dar, I was forced to go as I had arrived sick. It was the closest I have seen to my hometown Michigan hospital, recipient of the Malcom Baldridge Award for Quality, where every inpatient room is single. I became relieved that maybe for a non-emergency illness, I could survive in Tanzania.

Before returning to Lindi, I stocked up at my favorite pharmacy. For some reason, I feel more confident that his generics are not fake. The owner is a Tanzanian East Indian. The pharmacy shelves are stocked with familiar items: Tums, Listerine, dental floss, name brand vitamins. If I rattle off a name, if the pharmacist is not familiar, he quickly refers to his reference book. The staff seems knowledgeable and cordial, all a plus. I can buy name brand antibiotics made by my ex-employer for 34,000 TZS ($20) or the "equivalent" generic for 3,400 TZS. With time, I have learned to rely more on Lindi and whatever generics they have to offer. Dar is no longer a required trip.

I still travel to the States from time to time, so I book doctor's appointments for when I'm there. It is nice to be able to go back to a place I trust and feel comfortable in. I called my American doctor's office to make an appointment for a non-emergency physical. I was quickly reminded that I was dealing with *mzungus* when the receptionist had to get special permission to squeeze me in even though the appointment would be five months out.

She suggested calling thirteen months in advance next time. A bit of a hassle, but I do like physicians who work by appointment and keep to a schedule. It means they respect my time, and I must respect theirs. Upon making my appointment, my doctor immediately ordered the labs so she would have the results in advance. *Mzungu* healthcare for the *mzungu*. I was giddy.

It is as if my destiny was written the minute I met my soul mate and he introduced me to his country, his village, his homeland, his people—my people. It is just too bad that for a surgically menopausal woman, it is so darn hot and humid! I had to get a prescription at Aga Khan when my hormone replacement therapy (HRT) ran out.

Luckily, my favorite Dar pharmacist came through. He was able to supply the name brand tablets made by my ex-employer. The only problem was that my State-side doctor had just lowered my dose to an amount that is not available in Tanzania. That alone will keep me going to the States indefinitely.

Tanzania, especially Lindi, has a long way to go for preventive care and patient-doctor relationships. The overall life expectancy for those living in the Lindi region is 56.8 years. I did some internet search. For the years available, one source says there are 0.0 doctors per 1,000 people. (I think they must round to the nearest tenth.) Another source said 0.02 doctors per 1,000 people. The latter also reports 0.2 midwives or nurses per 1,000. There simply aren't enough healthcare professionals to go around.

Another issue is people's resistance to modern medicine. Many still go to traditional unlicensed bush healers. By the time they are done with the bush healers, the patient is extremely ill due to the delay. It is often too late once they make it to a government hospital. If it is not too late, they often cannot afford to buy the prescriptions they are given. There are government-supplied medicines that are supposed to be available at little to no cost, but they somehow end up in private pharmacies. I can only speculate how that happens.

If the people who wait until the last minute to come to the hospital are fortunate enough to get the required medicine, they may not follow the instructions. Consequently, mortality rates are high for those visiting the hospital; people get suspicious. They do not realize the delay and lack of preventive care are the real the problem.

I hope my destiny is to live a healthy life with my dear Saidi. It is hard to imagine one of us without the other. I pray for our good health every day. Compared to the average life expectancy in the Lindi region, Saidi and I, at age 56 and 58 years old respectively, are beating the odds.

CHAPTER 26

STAYING CONNECTED

A s much as I love Jome, sometimes it is nice to get a taste of what I left behind. I convinced Saidi one day to allow us to stay in a hotel that caters to Westerners. I didn't have to do much convincing really. I made a little joke out of it. "Hey, you have taught me how to poo in the bush, live with geckos, treat malaria, take cold or warm showers with a bucket, have intermittent power and conserve water. I have had a monkey in my *banda* and a rat in my bedroom. Can I please, dear, stay in a *mzungu* hotel?" He laughed. We decided to stay in the new Holiday Inn in Dar in city center. It has three restaurants and a business center—the works.

Even though I had a cold, I loved the food. At the breakfast buffet, I ate real cheese and yogurt, food you do not come by much in Tanzania. I also had delicious cakes (of course with a double es- presso) in the coffee shop. We ate twice at a locally owned restaurant with two American fellows, and we had Lebanese food with Nancy, the American volunteer intern.

We had a wonderful getaway, so when we had to stay an extra night because of our stalled car, I was not heartbroken. Sure, it broke our budget, but I loved every minute of it. We completed most of our to-do list while in Dar, including getting "Private Road," "Ruvu➔," and "Jome⬅" signs made. I also stocked up on malaria meds, antibiotics and de-worming meds for intestinal parasites. No prescription needed.

Our trips to Dar were more business than pleasure, but we became fixtures at the Holiday Inn over time. Thanks to the many rewards points we accumulated, we earned a free night. When we used it, we decided to upgrade to an executive suite. It was beautiful. We were living the good life—until we were awakened in the middle of the night by an announcement over the intercom, first in Swahili and then in English: "There is an emergency in the building. Please calmly evacuate immediately."

I was foggier than Saidi, so I didn't realize whose pants I was putting on. "You are wearing my jeans!" he said. I hurriedly changed, unsure of what was going on. "Hurry up," he said as he waited impatiently. "It could be a bomb!"

My mind raced as I grabbed our important belongings and rushed out of the room. Am I supposed to die this way? Who will ever know? We joined other frazzled guests in the hallway and took the fire escape nine stories down. When we arrived downstairs, a worker reassured us everything was OK. Apparently, a guest had been smoking in his room. We all let out a sigh of relief. The building was not on fire; we were not under a bomb threat; and a war had not been waged. Life would go on.

On the way back to the room, we shared the elevator with an elderly European couple who looked just as disheveled as we did. The woman's hair was standing up on end. In matters of survival, presentation becomes an afterthought. The things we typically value so much mean nothing when our lives are at stake.

As I got in bed and prepared to go back to sleep, I thought about my legacy. When I do finally leave this world, what will I be leaving behind? Perhaps that incident was a sign. Perhaps it planted in me the seed that later became LIFT.

On our one-year wedding anniversary, we decided to celebrate in Mtwara, a one-and-a-half-hour drive south. Fuel is expensive here, about twice the price in the US, so we wanted to minimize our trips to Dar. The entire road between Lindi and Mtwara is paved, so it was a smooth, uneventful ride. We stayed in a bungalow at a Swedish-owned beachside resort overlooking the Indian Ocean. The canopy of the brilliant blue East African sky enveloped us as we sat outside our bungalow, the ocean breeze sweeping across our skin. We watched the dhows and fisherman on the water and enjoyed each other's company. It was the perfect completion to the first year in my new life with my new husband.

The next day, we lunched at the Old Boma Hotel in Mikindani. It was built as a German fort 100 years ago. It is beautifully constructed of coral and limestone, a method that is now illegal due to its impact on the ecosystem. Mikindani has many old buildings that were built by Arabs long ago. It sits on a hill overlooking the Indian Ocean lagoon that famed explorer Dr. Livingston calls "the finest harbor on the coast." It is run by Trade Aid, a British charitable trust that aims to provide vocational education and employment in Mikindani. The rooms, most of which overlook the ocean or garden, are spacious and furnished with hand carved beds and *Tinga Tinga* art. It is a breathtaking place. Maybe we'll stay here for our next anniversary, we thought. We did stay there the following year. We were not disappointed.

Weekend getaways keep me connected to some of the Western amenities I am accustomed to, but the best way to keep connected to people has been through email and social media.

Initially, I only had access while in town. I would hurry through my 20 emails per day as Saidi drove around, running errands. Mobile service was scarce in Jome early on. We changed to a company more amenable to the bush, but we didn't see much difference. Eventually, we discovered we could get a one-bar signal on the north side of Jome if we stood on the rocks.

Knowing how important the internet is to me, Saidi explored the area for the optimum signal and decided to build a grass *banda* there. My tech savvy hero. Once a day, I would hike one kilometer to my internet café. The view was spectacular, but the connection crawled and was intermittent. Nevertheless, I was thrilled with the little peep it gave me into the world I had left.

While discussing my internet woes with an ex-colleague, he mentioned that a repeater could enhance my signal. Immediately, I began to scour the internet. I ordered the repeater and waited. After a hair-raising customs experience at the Dar airport, we picked up our new device. Uninterrupted internet service was on the way.

At Hasimi's suggestion, we hired a *fundi* to install it. The *fundi* had no idea how to install a repeater, but he figured it out with no problem. Without making any adjustments, we turned on the power and everyone looked at their phones. Full bars. Amazingly, I was able to connect to the internet on the first try. For me, the repeater offered the biggest quality of life enhancement. It made managing my personal affairs so much easier. I voted, paid bills, completed online courses to maintain my project management certification and even paid Uncle Sam.

With the internet working, the next leap into the 21st century was to buy an e-reader. I decided on a Kindle based on a recommendation from Nancy. I also liked that Amazon ships internationally. With my Kindle in hand, I was able to shop for and download books. Granted, I cannot watch YouTube videos on the network, but I do not mind that so much. Anything that requires high bandwidth has to be done in town, and updates that would take five minutes on a 3G network may take five hours in Jome. Nevertheless, I am connected.

Social media and emails help me stay in contact with family and friends, but nothing replaces a real face-to-face conversation. My current plan is to travel to the States every two years, but I wonder when the trips will become more sporadic. With each subsequent visit, my list of items to bring back gets shorter. I have gotten much better at surviving on the land, and things I thought I needed are no longer important.

I look forward to the day when my grandchildren will be able to visit their aging grandmother for their summer breaks, just as my daughter visited hers in Libya. The cycle of life continues.

CHAPTER 27

GOD WILLING

It's easy to be ungrateful. Perhaps it is part of the human condition. When I catch myself complaining, I stop and think of my many blessings. Yes, we had been getting more continuous rain than I had ever seen since I moved to Tanzania. Yes, our cistern was leaking, which meant we couldn't store any of the rain we were getting. Yes, it rained in the middle of our road that was being improved, leaving a muddy mess and making it virtually unpassable. Yes, our car was with a mechanic in town for a week, meaning we had no transportation. Yes, we had very little solar power because of the rain. Yes, we were low on diesel fuel for the generator. Yes, I had no bread and no fresh vegetables because I could not get to town. But *Alhamdulillah* (all praises to God), I had the ability to stock-up on food, a place to live, good health and a car to fix.

Though I missed my fresh veggies, I had rice and fresh beans, eggs from our chickens, pasta and tomato paste, Quaker Oats (yuck), coffee, tea, bottled water, juice and 7-UP. Saidi would sometimes complain when I bought groceries, but he now understands why I stock up on essentials. It was the longest we had ever been cut off, about 10 days, but we got through. I am thankful.

I have always been a risk taker. Nothing in life comes without taking a chance. I always ask myself, what is the worst thing that can happen, and can I live with the consequences if realized? I asked myself that question before moving and was prepared to face any consequences that could arise. Saidi wanted to come home to Jome where he fished and lived as a boy, where his father is buried. Though I had never been here, I wanted to come home, too.

It is as if my destiny was written the minute I met my soul mate and he introduced me to his country, his village, his homeland, his people—my people. I am at peace in Jome.

I have learned to make small talk with the fishermen and women who collect plants from the ocean to sell. I think they are more relaxed now that they realize we aren't here to disrupt their work. They are quicker to initiate conversation with me, but the children still stare, curious about the Black *mzungu*. That will probably never change. I'm OK with that now.

Luke, my Zimbabwean friend, wrote to me after one of his camping excursions in Jome:

"So much **potential**. How do we measure this word? In simple English, it means likely, probable, promising, do-able, achievable, feasible, viable, workable, and yes, my favourite one—in the cards. Of course, the opposite of all these words means impossible, but I do not believe in impossible. The promise of rain is now with us. The new earth smell, the essence of life, a new season, a new start, a new challenge, another beginning's end. We shall see that what will be, will be."

Insha'Allah.

By the time most people reach the age of 50, it is likely that they have loved and lost. They have probably experienced hope that was replaced by disappointment and betrayal. Saidi's and my stories are worlds apart, but they are also the same.

Before we met, we both had begun to settle into our memories of what could have been. Our story is a story of renewed hope, of everlasting faith. Every day I awake, I thank God for giving me this second chance in a place I could have only dreamed of years earlier.

Luke once wrote to me, "I find Jome's solitude part of a beautiful journey that fills my soul with reward... [It] tempers the 'what the hell am I doing in this part of the world?'" Well, Luke, I ask myself that question each day. Then, as I look at the sunrise each morning over the massive Indian Ocean with my morning coffee in hand, the birds and the voice of the ocean answer me.

The irony is that Jome's intense beauty is situated among extreme poverty. The challenges of life around us keep us from slipping into an intoxicating state of complacency. I struggle every day not to use my *mzungu* upbringing to judge, but instead to take in what the people have to offer and to teach me. I want it to be symbiotic, this relationship between Africa and me, each one giving, each one receiving.

Africa can test your patience. Yet, it is a land of people who have nothing but patience. Each animal teaches patience and persistence while waiting for its meal. Farmers hope the next season will bring rain so they can feed their families each day. They say, "If this is not the year, maybe next year, God willing." Though I accept I will always be different, I pray for the day when the *mzungu* title is no longer needed. If not this year, maybe next year, God willing.

GLOSSARY

AC- abbreviation for "alternate current."

Adhan- Muslim call to prayer.

Alhamdulillah- Arabic expression used by Muslims, meaning "All praises are due to God" or "Thanks to God."

As salaam alaikum- Muslim greeting meaning "Peace be upon you."

Bajaji- a three-wheeled economical scooter used as a taxi.

Banda- a small hut. Can be made of grass, mud, limestone or brick.

Bangi- Swahili for marijuana.

Bint- Swahili and Arabic word for daughter

Choo- Swahili word for toilet

Daladala- public transportation, usually privately operated for the general public. Can be a van or small bus.

Dhikri- literally is Arabic for "remembering Allah," but it is also a local ritual where Muslims gather to recite chants in remembrance of Allah or the Prophet Mohamed.

DC- abbreviation for "direct current."

Eid-ul-fitr- Muslim festival or holiday celebrating the end of the fasting month of *Ramadan*.

Fundi- Swahili for a craftsman or repairman.

Hajj- pilgrimage to Mecca required by all Muslims who can afford to do so.

Hakuna Matata –Swahili for "No worries."

Halal- used to refer to something that is permissible in Islam.

Haram- prohibited by Islamic law.

Hijab- head covering of Muslim women.

Hodi- Swahili for "May I come in"

Iftar- meal to break the daytime fast during the *Ramadan*.

Imam- Muslim cleric; also used for the leader of congregational Muslim prayer.

Insha'Allah - Arabic for "God willing."

Iyat- a verse from the Quran.

Jando - a ceremony of young boys in which they are circumcised.

Jinn- an Islamic concept, an unseen being that is like human in their duties to God.

Jome- name given by Saidi's father, Mohamed Masudi, for the area he settled.

Kanga- a large piece of brightly printed cloth used as a garment by East African women.

Karibu- Swahili for welcome.

Kenge- Swahili for monitor lizard.

Khutbah- sermon given in the mosque for Friday prayer.

Kiputiputi- butterfly in the local dialect.

Kizunguzungu- Swahili for dizzy.

LIFT- Lindi Islamic Foundation of Tanzania.

Madrasa - Arabic word for "school," but also used to refer to Islamic Schools.

Marahaba- return greeting for Shikamoo of an elder to a younger person.

Mchanga- Swahili for sand.

Minbar- area that the Friday sermons are given from in a mosque, analogous to a church pulpit.

Muezzin- person that makes Adhan.

Mwani- Swahili for a type of seaweed harvested as a cash crop.

Mzee- Swahili for elderly person.

Mzungu- literally is the Swahili word for "wanderer," but it is usually used to denote a person of European descent or a foreigner.

NGO- abbreviation for Non-government organization.

PBUH- abbreviation for "peace be upon him," a respectful term Muslim use after mentioning Prophet Mohamed.

Pipi- Swahili for candy.

Pikepike- Swahili for motorcycle.

Pole- Swahili for sorry.

Polepole- Swahili for slowly.

Rakat - a repetition of the complete act of prostration during the Muslim prayer.

Ramadan- ninth month on the Muslim lunar calendar. It is also the fasting month for Muslims and a time of heightened worship. The Quran was first revealed during this month.

Sadaqa- voluntary charity for Muslims.

Salaam- Arabic word for peace. It is also used as a greeting to mean that all is well.

Samaki- Swahili for fish.

Shikamoo- respectful greeting given by a younger person to and older person. There is no direct translation.

SWT- abbreviation for "Subhanahu Wa Ta'ala," or "Glory to Him, the Exalted." Muslims use these or similar words to glorify God when mentioning His name.

Surah- a chapter in the Holy Quran

Tawaweer- congregational night prayers conducted during the holy Muslim month of *Ramadan.*

Tinga Tinga- a type of Tanzanian artwork, known for its bright colors. Popular with tourists.

TZS- Tanzanian Schilling.

Ugali- a dough-like food made from cooked flour.

Unga –Swahili for flour.

Wa alaikum wa salaam- return greeting to "As salaamu alaikum." In Arabic means "And Peace be Upon You."

Wali- Swahili for cooked rice. Also Arabic for guardian.

Wazee- plural of mzee.

ALSO FROM NIYAH

BOOKS

Jihad of the Soul: Singlehood and the Search for Love in
Muslim America (Zarinah El-Amin Naeem)
The Spiritual Adam by Imam Abdullah El-Amin
The Little Book of Marriage Advice

CALENDARS

Beautifully Wrapped: The Fashion, Tradition, and Culture of
Headwrapping

Arabic Calligraffiti: The Street Art of El Seed

FORTHCOMING

Headwrapping 101: 20 Basic Styles to get you Beautifully Wrapped
The Power of Dua by Zahara Smith

EXHIBITS

Beautifully Wrapped: The Fashion Tradition, and Culture of
Headwrapping Photography Exhibition

EXCERPT FROM STUDY GUIDE

More questions can be found at www.TheBlackMzungu.com

The BLACK MZUNGU's discussion of identity, colonization, love, trust, poverty and more is a wonderful platform to engage and spark deep meaningful conversations. Here are a few questions to use in your group discussion.

1. What type of events in someone's life might make someone move to another part of the world?

2. What burden do African Americans carry that make some consider a connection to a continent they never visited? Should they?

3. What common bond is more important in forming friendships: religion, color, language, socio-economic, nationality?

4. What comforts could you sacrifice to make a new life? And, what would you need to replace those comforts?

5. Do you think the author will live out her life in her new home? If not, what would cause her to return back to the States permanently?

6. What are the possible repercussions of reporting an illegal activity that seems systemic and accepted by society?

7. What boundaries would you set with you neighbors? When do you give and when do you decline? Are you more apt to give if someone asks?

8. Africa is rich in resources. Why has its wealth not improved the lives of the masses? What changes, if any, need to be made for the people of southeast Tanzania to benefit from the discovery of natural gas?

ABOUT THE AUTHOR

Alexandria Osborne was born in 1956 in Harlem, New York and graduated from the Bronx High School of Science. After earning a B.S. in Chemistry from Pratt Institute in Brooklyn, New York, Alex accepted a position at a global pharmaceutical company in Kalamazoo, Michigan.

Michigan brought about many life changes including marriage to a Libyan American, and converting to Islam. It's also the place Alex raised her daughter, Zubayda with whom she would often travel to Libya. Finding it difficult to say Alex, her Libyan in-laws gave her the name Nur, a name she adopted as her own. It was the beginning of a dynamic, cross-cultural life.

In 2005, Nur earned a MBA in Management from Western Michigan University and later began her studies for a PhD in Management with a specialty in Leadership and Organization Change. In 2009, she made her first visit to sub-Sahara Africa to begin a six-month fellowship for an international NGO in Tanzania. That same year, her research study conducted at Tripoli Medical Center in Libya was approved, earning her a PhD from Walden University.

During her fellowship, she met her current husband, Saidi, and returned to his homeland in the coastal southern region of Lindi, Tanzania. In 2013, she founded the Lindi Islamic Foundation of Tanzania–LIFT (www.tanzania-lift.org). She now lives in Tanzania with her husband, their chickens and other farm animals. She enjoys starting off each morning with a good strong cup of Tanzanian coffee.

LINDI ISLAMIC FOUNDATION OF TANZANIA

The unsolicited generosity I received after sharing pictures and stories from Tanzania (first as a requirement of my fellowship, and later as a personal interest) was heartwarming. I received various types of charity from around the world for the people of my village and surrounding areas.

It is this generosity that inspired the formation of the Lindi Islamic Foundation of Tanzania (LIFT). After 3 years of receiving donations for distribution to communities in the Lindi region, it soon became apparent that this charity is not just a one-time contribution. Therefore, LIFT was founded and organized to ensure that the charity targeted for the most vulnerable in the Lindi Region can continue. By engaging community members and leaders from within Lindi region, LIFT will InshaAllah (God Willing) be an organization that can "LIFT" the most vulnerable to a place where they can be self-sufficient and have access to those things that many of us take for granted: food, healthcare, education, water, sanitation, and spiritual growth.

Jazakallahu khairan (May God reward you with good).

Alexandria Osborne, PhD, PMP
(also known as Dr. Nur)

www.tanzania-lift.org

CPSIA information can be obtained
at www.ICGtesting.com
Printed in the USA
LVOW11s1154191116
513696LV00002B/448/P